THE

ACCOUNTABLE

ORGANIZATION

THE

ACCOUNTABLE

ORGANIZATION

Reclaiming Integrity,
Restoring Trust

JOHN MARCHICA

PALO ALTO, CALIFORNIA

Published by Davies-Black Publishing, a division of CPP, Inc., 3803 East Bayshore Road, Palo Alto, CA 94303; 800-624-1765.

Special discounts on bulk quantities of Davies-Black books are available to corporations, professional associations, and other organizations. For details, contact the Director of Marketing and Sales at Davies-Black Publishing; 650-691-9123; fax 650-623-9271.

Davies-Black and colophon are registered trademarks of CPP, Inc. *Myers-Briggs Type Indicator,* Myers-Briggs, and MBTI are trademarks or registered trademarks of the Myers-Briggs Type Indicator Trust in the United States and other countries. Eudora is a registered trademark of QUALCOMM Incorporated. iTunes is a registered trademark and iPod is a trademark of Apple Computer, Inc. Windows is a registered trademark of Microsoft Corporation. Tylenol is a registered trademark of Johnson & Johnson.

Visit the Davies-Black Publishing web site at www.daviesblack.com.

08 07 06 05 04   10 9 8 7 6 5 4 3 2 1
Printed in the United States of America

Library of Congress Cataloging-in-Publication Data
Marchica, John.
   The accountable organization : reclaiming integrity, restoring trust /
John Marchica.— 1st ed.
     p. cm.
   Includes bibliographical references and index.
   ISBN 0-89106-185-1 (hardcover)
   1. Social responsibility of business. 2. Business ethics. I. Title.
   HD60.M3647 2004
   658.4′08—dc22

                                   2003028302

FIRST EDITION
First printing 2004

For Antonio, Michael, and Gabriela.
In memory of Tom Richardson.

CONTENTS

Acknowledgments   ix

About the Author   xiii

Foreword   xv

Introduction   xxi

ONE   Trust: Understanding Its Importance at Eye Level   1

TWO   Accountability: Taking Responsibility for Choices   15

THREE   Integrity: Doing the Right Thing   27

FOUR   Purpose: Clarifying What You Stand For   43

FIVE   Execution: Implementing Strategy with
         Commitment and Discipline   63

SIX	Leadership: Navigating Context, Fulfilling Many Roles	73
SEVEN	Communication: Connecting Effectively and with Empathy	97
EIGHT	Conflict: Seeking Resolution Through Preparation and Negotiation	119
NINE	Risk: Breaking Barriers Creatively and Courageously	139
TEN	Southwest Airlines: Integrating Accountable Organization Principles	159
	Conclusion	175
	Notes	181
	Bibliography	189
	Index	193

ACKNOWLEDGMENTS

As anyone who has written a book will attest, attempting to acknowledge all of those who have influenced the process is an impossible exercise. This book is a culmination of experiences; every day I continue to work on and learn from my personal and professional relationships. In one way or another, all of the important people in my life have contributed to my understanding of the topics in this book.

My wife, Cristina, was the first to celebrate with me when I first received an agreement from Davies-Black Publishing to write *The Accountable Organization*. (Neither of us knew at the time what I was getting into—but ask either one of us, and we'd do it again.) Some authors have compared writing books to raising children. Well, our three children were all under the age of five during the writing of this book, and I thank my wife for all the extra hours and support she provided while I was tapping away on my PowerBook. Cristina, amid our frenetic lives and a house full of toddlers, you never once doubted me—and for that I am eternally grateful.

This project was conceived and completed collaboratively with Elisa Gueffier, my close friend and long-time FWI writer/editor. Elisa provided much of the research and interview transcriptions, and, thankfully, prodded me through frustrating bouts of writer's block. She skillfully edited my often-disconnected thoughts and, through countless, patient hours of feedback, helped me to become a better writer. I am grateful to Elisa for her constant encouragement and for her tireless work in helping to complete this book. I've never met a better writer, or one who sets the bar for personal excellence so high.

Thanks to my publishing consultant and agent, Roland Elgey, for his wisdom, guidance, and support in helping this book make it to market. Roland was present in all the early meetings for the book, ensured that we found the right publishing partner, and provided invaluable guidance throughout the process.

My parents, John and Emily Marchica, helped me to understand at a very early age the importance of honesty and honor. And beyond even what parents provide, throughout the years they've given me unwavering support. I thank my brother, Ray, for being there in the most difficult of times, and for providing an important role model for guerilla entrepreneurship. Christina, more a sister than sister-in-law, is a constant reminder of the power of determination and courage. And in so many ways, the rest of my extended family—Cassandra, Dominic, Angelia, Dario, Carlos, Frank, Art, Eva, and others—have shown me how *The Accountable Organization* has meaning in life as well as in business.

I'm indebted to the people of FWI—both past and present—for all the work they do, for their tireless efforts in producing a terrific product. I've learned many lessons in leadership through our shared experience of growing a company. I hope that they, too, have enjoyed the ride.

I owe special gratitude to my friends and mentors James Newton, Michael and Michelle Saul, Bev Foster, Sue Muck, and Lauryn Rice. They helped me to understand the true importance of accountability and integrity in business and in life, and why this was a topic that deserved a book.

I'd further like to acknowledge the many reviewers of *The Accountable Organization*, whose insights helped crystallize my thinking: Brendan Baker, Stephen Chavez, Sandy Costa, Don Harmon, Alan Hirshman, Don Lorenzen, Cristina Marchica, John D. Marchica, Brett McClain, Fred Prillaman, Tom Rough, Allison Smith, Lucian Spataro, Stacey Vrbas, David Wolfenden, and Keven Zeigler.

Additionally, thanks to those who have provided crucial support to me at various points in my business experience, especially Steve Achenbach, John Adams, Bob Allard, Bob Altman, Roy Andersen, Karlene Arnold, Debby Baker, Haley Balzano, Gene Barinholtz, Trish Bear, Arthur Bill, Frank Bill,

Bob Bingham, Chris Bleck, Grant Bogle, Brian Bowen, Phil Breidenbach, Craig Budwitz, Bruce Bunyan, Larry Carbone, Cristina Carlino, Bill Carlson, Ole Carlson, Bill Chase, Sue Cisco, Steve Cohn, Peter Conradi, Troy Darling, Deryk David, Tom Dee, John Del Giorno, Mike Denning, Jan Fisher, Scott Flanders, Paul Foulger, Bob Gear, Martin Gilligan, Dave Goffredo, Jeffrey Gossrow, Dane Hartung, Craig Hedges, John Hines, John Kadlic, Bob Kelly, Chris Keubler, Mike Killion, Louis Kirby, Tom Knight, Barry Labinger, Tom Larson, Dave Lee, Steve Levine, Cheryl Lubbert, Tom Markey, Rick Martin, Suzanne McDonald, Arlene Meyers, Mary Michael, David Misiak, Mike Motto, David Murphy, David Newbart, Jamie Ogle, Tip Parker, Jeff Parkhill, Blasine Penkowski, Audrey Petty, Nhat Phung, Laura Piel, Steve Pittendrigh, Rick Plotz, Jonathan Pochyly, John Powers, Chau Pyatt, Julio Quintana, Jeffrey Rausch, John Richter, Gary Ruben, Susan Rudolphi, Frank Schab, Susan Scott, Raymond Spencer, Tim Spooner, Steve Steiber, Pat Stoner, Richard Stout, Dan Sullivan, Chris and Jana Valle, Khristen Vanderwey, John Vehr, Tom Watkins, Craig Weber, Andrew Welch, Jerry Wenker, and Steve Williams. Each of you has influenced the ideas in this book, even if in the moment you didn't know it.

This book wouldn't have been possible without the commitment and dedication of Davies-Black Publishing, especially my editor, Connie Kallback; Laura Simonds, director of marketing and sales; and Lee Langhammer Law, publisher. Mark Chambers skillfully provided final editing and proofing.

ABOUT THE AUTHOR

John Marchica is founder and CEO of FWI, a medical information services provider based in Scottsdale, Arizona, that has been named twice to the *Inc.* 500 list of America's fastest-growing private companies. He has been recognized as a finalist for the Ernst & Young Entrepreneur of the Year Award and was among the youngest chairs named by TEC, the international business coaching and peer-group organization for CEOs. A frequent keynote speaker on trust-based marketing and the principles presented in *The Accountable Organization*, he holds a B.A. degree in economics from Knox College, an M.A. degree in public policy from the University of Chicago, and an M.B.A. degree, also from the University of Chicago. His web site can be found at www.johnmarchica.com.

FOREWORD

Early in this book, John Marchica asks, "Should we rely on law to stand in for integrity?" As a legislator, this question is of particular interest to me—it's reminiscent of an old political saw, one that says you can't legislate morality. Of course, that doesn't mean we won't try.

In my first session as a member of the Illinois General Assembly, we passed several measures designed to impose integrity and accountability on corporations operating in the state. Not surprisingly, these laws were passed in direct response to Enron, WorldCom, and a host of other—more local—episodes of corporate misbehavior. To be fair, I expect these measures will make companies doing business in Illinois behave better. They will not, however, make corporations any more ethical or accountable or full of integrity. This is not a failure of the laws we enacted; it is merely a consequence of the inherent difference between laws and ethics.

Laws are external rules imposed by society to discourage undesirable behavior. Laws influence behavior by prescribing imminent consequences, be they imprisonment or monetary penalties. But laws are enforceable only when society in some way observes or documents the bad behavior.

Ethics are quite different from laws. Ethics are similarly intended to discourage undesirable behavior, but they are internal rules that extend much further into the gray area between "right" and "wrong"—an area we largely ignore in defining "legal" versus "illegal" activities. Ethics influence behavior too, of course, but not through the threat of imminent punishment. The consequences of unethical behavior are far more ethereal—damage to one's reputation, perhaps, or an unfortunate fate in the afterlife, if that is consistent with one's religious beliefs. Most important, we as individuals enforce our own ethics, following our own internal compass. In other words, while laws are enforced by an observant society, ethics are—to paraphrase another old saw—the principles that guide our behavior when no one else is watching. An ethical person would be troubled by his or her own unethical behavior, even (or especially) if it remains a secret taken to the grave; an unethical person, on the other hand, may be troubled not at all by his unethical behavior, provided that no one ever finds out.

Why is the theoretical difference between laws and ethics relevant to a commercial organization? Businesses, after all, operate in a legally defined marketplace. In most cases, adherence to law is all that many folks expect of business enterprises. Some professionals—for example, lawyers and doctors—impose upon themselves supralegal codes of conduct that define ethical expectations for members. Beyond these laws and professional codes, however, there is no common system of ethics that governs business relationships. But perhaps there should be.

This notion, I think, is John Marchica's great contribution in writing *The Accountable Organization*. Companies should be ethical, should be accountable, should be full of integrity—not just because it's right, but because it's smart business. As John shows, Accountable Organizations have a competitive advantage over companies without a robust ethical foundation.

We want to live in a world where we can, with some reliability, predict how others will behave in given circumstances; we want to have confidence in our expectations of others. Laws and ethics are imperfect but complementary attempts to create that world. And the efficient operation of a sustainable business enterprise demands no less.

So, how do we infuse organizations with the sort of ethical principles required for the efficient conduct of business? Like John, I am a father of young children, and as a consequence of fatherhood (or perhaps because of cumulative sleep deprivation) too many of my analogies these days revolve around rearing children. Nonetheless, here I think the analogy is instructive: We infuse business organizations with ethical principles in the same way that we infuse children with ethical principles—holistically, by example, by instruction, by practice, by failure, and by success.

In *The Accountable Organization*, John provides us with a road map for making our organizations accountable, for making them ethical—and it is a good road map. As a legislator, my "business" is really nothing more than *being accountable* to the people who elected me. I need not turn a profit, I need not produce a product, I need not do anything other than *be accountable*. And with the turn of almost every page of this book, I find myself responding viscerally to John's ideas, preparing in my head some other way I could be more accountable to my constituents, or fretting about some opportunity I had missed to be accountable. In short, while John's book is especially well tailored to the CEOs of the corporate world, it transcends such narrow application—this book is essential reading for anyone who must organize a human enterprise, who must (willingly or unwillingly) assume the responsibility of "leader."

I'm not surprised that John chose to write this book at this moment in time. I've known John for almost twenty years, and I've watched him grow into ever-larger and more challenging leadership roles. I have always admired his quiet integrity and his evolving ability to lead with grace and humility. In recent years, our conversations have often turned to the public failures of corporate America, and I have sensed in John a growing frustration and disappointment. In typical fashion, John has channeled that frustration not into a scathing indictment of corporate leaders, but rather into a blueprint for change. It is John's intellectual ju-jitsu, his ability to turn negatives into positives, that makes him a success in business and in life.

Years ago, when John was preparing to launch his company, he and I talked regularly about his plans, his prospects, and the personal and professional risks he faced. Truth be told, few of us, faced with the opportunity, would refuse a generous and regular paycheck in favor of the speculative returns of true entrepreneurship. Despite the risks, despite the uncertainties, John did just that, and—in no small part because of his integrity—he did it with remarkable success.

John's success came as no surprise to those of us "who knew him when." In recounting the launch of his company, John notes that he was able to do so without any outside financial help, without any venture capital, without even asking any friends to invest a dollar or two. I was finishing law school at the time—deep in debt and with little money in my pocket, much less for investments. Had John asked, however, I would have borrowed against my car, hocked my guitar, done whatever I had to do to invest in his company. Part of me still wishes that he had asked. But the truth is that I've been afforded a far richer opportunity than investing in John's company—I've had the rare privilege of investing in John, and having him invest in me. The returns—such as reading this book and writing this foreword—are far more rewarding.

Don Harmon
Illinois State Senator
September 2003

INTRODUCTION

The idea of writing *The Accountable Organization* came to me soon after I led FaxWatch, Inc. (FWI), the medical information services company I founded, through a rebranding process. The deep introspection I undertook helped me to identify more than just a new name and logo for our company—in the process, I identified the underlying principles that would set us apart from our competition and fuel our continued growth and success.

Many people wait a lifetime to chronicle what they learned in business. As an entrepreneur with a still-young company, I wanted to offer something unique, a different perspective from the rest. But, like countless others, I was infuriated by the corporate chicanery going on in America. It seemed like every day another chief executive was going down in flames. And when Arthur Andersen fell, it was a wake-up call. I had long respected Andersen for what I believed were its ethical standards and quality of work. If it could be taken down, no company was safe.

Amid all the talk of restoring trust in corporate America, it became clear that legislation and litigation would not be enough to get us there. The change had to be initiated by those who had the most at stake: the people at the companies themselves. But what would that change look like? In other words, what kinds of organizations foster trust, both within and without? To answer this question, I drew on the lessons I'd learned from my experiences in corporate America and as an entrepreneur and CEO. I interviewed people across industries and job functions, from CEOs to frontline managers.

I found that to earn trust, a company must be founded on integrity and embrace accountability—it must be what I call an Accountable Organization. Chapters 1–3 in this book explore the foundational elements that are crucial in creating this kind of company.

Trust, however, isn't the only reward. An Accountable Organization also has a competitive advantage over firms without a strong ethical core. Here are some of the reasons why:

- Members of an Accountable Organization stand by ethical principles and create a meaningful purpose for their company—thus, they make better decisions. Because the ethical framework has been clearly articulated, there is less confusion over which path to take: decisions are made confidently based on what's *right*. Without this framework, decisions are often based on expediency or "what's-in-it-for-me" thinking—not the best strategy for ensuring the long-term sustainability of the business.

• Members of an Accountable Organization execute better. They establish systems and processes to reinforce accountability, including effective communication and conflict management. In contrast, organizations that communicate poorly or lack accountability are often riddled with internal conflict, confused priorities, and disconnected employees— translating into lower productivity and higher operational costs.

• Members of an Accountable Organization are strong, ethical leaders who embrace their greater responsibility to the organization as a whole. They understand the importance of taking risks for fueling creativity and innovation. Companies without accountable leadership will drift—or worse, be led astray—while those that avoid risk taking will stagnate.

• An Accountable Organization attracts more customers and keeps them longer. Customers know that principle-driven companies stand behind their products. They know what to expect in terms of quality and service. In short, people buy from companies—and people—they trust. Companies that neglect building trust-based relationships find themselves competing for fair-weather customers, result-ing in higher customer acquisition costs and increased customer defection.

- Finally, an Accountable Organization attracts and retains higher-caliber employees who won't stay at a company that doesn't have a strong moral fiber. As with customers, it's less costly to retain good employees than it is to hire new ones. Companies with lower ethical standards will have higher employee turnover, increased training costs, and lower productivity. In contrast, an Accountable Organization will attract and retain the best leaders, man-agers, and support staff.

Of course, market conditions, competitive forces, business strategy, capitalization, public policy, and many other variables influence whether a business succeeds or fails. Nonetheless, the strength of a company's culture makes an enormous difference when it comes to its balance sheet. For example, as this book's case study shows, Southwest Airlines' long-term success is not due solely to its being a "low-price" carrier—plenty of bargain-basement airlines have been forced out of markets by larger players. Rather, Southwest's long-term success has much to do with the "Warrior Spirit" of its employees—a culture that has provided Southwest with a lower cost structure and a com-pelling value proposition compared to its industry counterparts.

Accountable Organizations such as Southwest prosper in our free-market system because of the trust they earn. These companies are built on integrity, that is, adherence to core values, assumed to be moral and beneficial to both the organization and its stakeholders. Yet integrity in and of itself does not magically create trust. The organization must prove that its actions and choices are in alignment with its core values and deliver on this implied contract at every level.

Those who are skeptical about the government's power to improve matters are onto something. This framework—the relationship between integrity, accountability, and trust—cannot be conjured into existence through new laws or yet more lawsuits. Rather, it requires commitment at an individual level on every rung of the ladder *within* the organization itself. Unquestionably, it's unrealistic to believe that, say, forty thousand employees will simply adopt an accountable perspective on their own. The company's infrastructure plays a crucial role, as does organizational buy-in, often initiated by both formal and informal leaders. Therefore, *The Accountable Organization* seeks to help inspire individual commitment with concepts that are practical and actionable.

Purpose. Members of an Accountable Organization must first define what they stand for and where they are going. Without this understanding, a company allows itself to be steered by expediency rather than taking control of its own course. Chapter 4 addresses the vital importance of identifying an organization's values and purpose.

Execution. Once defined, an Accountable Organization's values and purpose are integrated into a robust strategic plan. This focused road map for execution provides clarity and specificity, defining performance standards and providing a common frame of reference for individual and organizational accountability. With the plan in place, what remains is effective implementation, which is addressed in chapter 5.

Leadership. Accountability means that a firm's leaders—not unlike elected officials in a democratic society—are responsible to the people they serve and should account for what they do on their behalf. While everyone in a company should be fully accountable, the leadership of the organization has an even greater responsibility, if only because their decisions and actions have greater impact. Chapter 6 discusses the different ways that CEOs are accountable to their organizations, primarily through the many essential roles they play.

Communication. When communication is incomplete or misleading, or when it shuts down completely, cynicism can creep into the culture. In contrast, effective and empathetic communication not only ensures organizational efficiency, it also builds trust. Chapter 7 shows how stakeholders in an Accountable Organization seek to establish communication that is clear, consistent, and compassionate, both internally and externally.

Conflict. When conflicts arise in the workplace, those involved often seek to assign blame, choosing to ignore their own part in the situation. Our desire to be "right" makes it difficult to see that we're in fact part of the problem. Chapter 8 provides insight on how to manage challenging situations—and how to remain accountable in the process.

Risk. Innovation and a competitive edge are necessary for a company to succeed. As such, leaders and other stakeholders must be willing to take educated, responsible risks. Chapter 9 looks at how the creativity and courageous decision making inherent in this kind of risk taking are crucial to the vitality of an Accountable Organization.

At the end of each chapter is a section entitled "Building the Accountable Organization" that includes questions to help you examine these topics on your own. You might even consider introducing these questions to prompt discussion in meetings. To best use this book, apply the lessons you find valuable to your current position, your state of business, and your organizational challenges.

Chapter 10 is a portrait of one Accountable Organization: Southwest Airlines. While the company has been profiled before, Southwest's continued success is even more remarkable now, given the abysmal state of the airline industry. This case study, featuring the insight of Southwest president and COO Colleen Barrett, demonstrates how the airline's stellar performance wouldn't have been possible without its unique culture.

Becoming an Accountable Organization is an ambitious proposition, but one that is realistic—and, in the end, a challenge worth undertaking. In the face of continual tests, members of Accountable Organizations work tenaciously to stay the course. They stand by their principles; lead with humility, compassion, and resolve; are fully accountable for their choices; and build steadfast trust among customers and fellow stakeholders. When individuals make this kind of commitment to reclaiming integrity and embracing accountability, the combined result is restored trust and long-term success.

So, whether you're a CEO, a manager, or a frontline employee, I urge you to take on the challenge of building an Accountable Organization. The rewards and fulfillment will come from the journey itself . . . not the destination.

I wish you success.

CHAPTER ONE

TRUST
Understanding Its Importance at Eye Level

At the end of July 2002, President Bush signed the Sarbanes-Oxley Act, a corporate corruption bill designed to reform business practices and reassure employees and shareholders. The president declared, "This law says to every American: there will not be a different ethical standard for Corporate America than the standard that applies to everyone else."[1] Among other items, Sarbanes-Oxley requires that publicly traded companies institute a code of ethics for their executive teams. As of this writing, large companies are scrambling to comply with the new inch-thick legislation, ostensibly enacted to restore public trust in American business.

A Crisis of Confidence

Enron. WorldCom. Arthur Andersen. These names and others are now associated with greed, mismanagement, and dishonesty. And despite claims to the contrary, it now appears that the few "bad apples" have tainted the bunch—at least when it comes to public perception. In a poll conducted in the summer of 2002, people ranked stockbrokers and CEOs of large corporations down at the bottom of the list of individuals who can be trusted, joining HMO managers and car dealers.[2]

How did we get here? In trying to make sense out of the crisis of confidence in American business, many point to the greatest stock market boom in U.S. history—capped in the late 1990s by the dot-com bubble. "Corporate responsibility is mainly a matter of attitudes, and the attitudes got corrupted by the mentality of the markets in the 1990s," former Federal Reserve Board Chairman Paul Volcker told *BusinessWeek.* "We went from 'greed is good' being said as a joke to people thinking that 'greed is good' was a fundamental fact."[3] Everyone wanted to join the party, and with good reason. The Dow more than tripled in five years, rising from approximately 3,600 in 1994 to a peak of over 11,700 in January 2000. The tech-heavy Nasdaq rocketed from just over 1,000 at the end of 1995 to break 5,000 in March 2000. Alan Greenspan's warning of "irrational exuberance" became something of a rallying cry.

It seemed like there was nowhere to go but up. I certainly wasn't immune to the euphoria. I founded my company in 1994, just as the market was really blasting off. I remember watching what was going on with mixed emotions. One part of me was envious—I watched the insta-millionaires sprouting up around me like weeds and wondered why I couldn't be one myself. I also was disappointed that going it on one's own, embracing the adventure of entrepreneurship, wasn't such a unique thing anymore. Everybody was doing it.

My company, FWI, is a provider of medical information services. FWI has always been privately held, with no angel investors or venture capital. Don't think, however, that the Internet frenzy didn't make me consider it. There was the rise of health care portals such as MedScape and Dr.Koop.com (the latter of which, once valued in the millions of dollars, was later sold for under $200,000). There was also the potential increase in competition—suddenly, anyone with a computer and an Internet connection was a publisher. The pressure was so great that at one point I considered changing the name of my company to FaxWatch.com.

At the same time, it was quite a rush. I bought stocks such as Amazon.com and watched them fly. But the party couldn't last forever. The pundits who said that the old rules of business and economics didn't apply anymore—after all, look at those valuations!—were wrong. It's not that society wasn't changed by the Internet, or that consumers didn't behave differently in this new environment. It's just that business is business. At some point, you need to make a profit or the market will punish you. Investors won't wait around forever as you hope to make money.

And in 2000, investors stopped waiting around. After reaching 5,000 territory in March, the Nasdaq composite index closed the year down by half; meanwhile, the Dow ended the year down 1,000 points from its peak. By midsummer 2002, the Dow had tumbled 32 percent from its high while the Nasdaq was down a frightening 74 percent. In the wake of the corporate scandals, both indices dropped below their post–September 11 lows.

During the meltdown, Alan Greenspan coined another phrase to sum up the times: "infectious greed." The Fed chairman noted that it was a difference of opportunity, not a fundamental shift in human nature, that was responsible for the scandals. "It is not that humans have become any more greedy than in generations past," he said. "It is that the avenues to express greed had grown so enormously."[4]

Greenspan's words aren't very comforting. According to him, greed will likely win, given the opportunity. And, according to the cynics, opportunities will always be found. But the Internet boom also has affected the direct relationship between consumers and companies. Consumers are now much better educated about the products they purchase. Rumors and bad news are spread instantaneously. Consumers have access to a truly global marketplace, vastly increasing competition. Finally, the promise of a new kind of workplace—embodied by the dot-com company and widely covered by the media—has gone largely unfulfilled.

Trust at Eye Level

It's no great leap to suggest that the recent scandals have contributed to the erosion of trust in business. While we're not naïve enough to think that our institutions are entirely free of unscrupulous behavior, many of us feel that a basic understanding is being violated. As an entrepreneur, I am a firm believer in the promise and opportunity of our free-market system. I also believe there is a fundamental level of trust necessary to sustain that system, a trust that has been subverted by an unscrupulous few—with, as we have seen, very damaging effects.

Noted social scientist Francis Fukuyama defines trust as an expectation among people that stems from "regular, honest, and cooperative behavior" and is based on "commonly shared norms." In his book *Trust: The Social Virtues and the Creation of Prosperity,* Fukuyama argues that "high-trust" societies such as the United States, with its capacity for forming spontaneous communities and associations, have been at the forefront of the global economy and wealth creation. Fukuyama warns, however, that distrust in America is on the rise. As evidence he cites the breakdown of families, churches, neighborhoods, and workplaces, as well as the increase in crime and litigation.[5]

In the larger context of American culture, public trust in institutional leadership has taken a beating in the last fifty years. In the 1960s and 1970s it was challenged by the Kennedy assassination, Vietnam, and Watergate. In more recent times, the public has seen a presidential impeachment, questions of due process in the O.J. Simpson trial, revelations of sex abuse in the Catholic Church, and uncertainty over terrorism and war.

So our high-trust society is being tested, and not just by the recent corporate scandals. In many real and disturbing ways, our expectations of "regular, honest, and cooperative behavior" have been betrayed. Inevitably, these betrayals erode the faith we put in institutions.

But what about our trust in each other, or what I'd call "eye-level" trust? How do we understand its role in our daily lives, relationships, and work?

In civilized society, some eye-level trust is assumed. This trust underlies everyday interactions between strangers, like taking a cab ride in an unfamiliar city. In our daily encounters with people, we trust that they will act in a way that is in our best interests—or at least isn't harmful to us. We don't have the time or the reason to form deeper relationships with most of the people we meet as we go about the smaller business of life, but we all have an understanding that everything will run smoother if we operate at a basic level of trust in each other.

But when we look at the relationships in which we have a lot at stake—such as business relationships—we can't assume that eye-level trust will simply "be there." Raymond Spencer is chairman and CEO of Kanbay Inc., a global systems integrator that provides high-value, technology-based business solutions. The company, named one of *ComputerWorld* magazine's "Best

Places to Work in IT," prides itself on being a "values-driven" organization. Spencer notes, "I think the question of trust is more on the forefront of people's minds today, not as assumed but as something that you in a sense have to earn, and which is very easily lost. Something in the past that might have been quickly forgiven . . . now can almost totally ruin a relationship."[6] As Spencer points out, this trust is a kind of knowledge, something we learn to be true through experience.

Spencer notes the great importance of building this eye-level trust with the clients at service-based Kanbay. "All we are is people," he says. "And the only asset we have, really, beyond their skill, is the asset of trust." Bob Bingham, CEO of The Little Gym, Inc., would agree. Through its franchises, The Little Gym offers curriculum-based, physical skill-building programs for children. "When you drop off your child with someone, you can't *almost* trust them, you have to have 100 percent trust in them," Bingham says. "And so trust is very much a part of what Little Gym is to the end consumer. Our obligation is to make sure that everyone who is delivering our product is completely well trained and qualified to do so."[7]

Like Kanbay and The Little Gym, trust is at the very core of what my own company, FWI, offers to its customers. FWI delivers timely, concise briefs on the latest developments in medical research and the industry to hundreds of thousands of physicians, health care executives, and patients. However, we are not a news organization in the traditional sense because much of our work is underwritten by corporate clients—primarily health care companies.

These companies hire FWI to provide information services for their customers. For example, a pharmaceutical company may underwrite a newsletter designed specifically for cardiologists. Every week, FWI sends these cardiologists a concise update on the most important research and other news affecting their practice. It is important that the sponsoring company have no editorial control over the information that the cardiologists receive from FWI—that the information we provide be objective and unbiased. Thus, the pharmaceutical company builds trust with those cardiologists through a genuine commitment to improving patient care by offering relevant continuing education. So, one can say that FWI is in the business of building trust through information. Thus, our product—and by extension, our brand—must stand for integrity and quality. For if the FWI brand doesn't earn trust with our readership, it ceases to have value . . . and the company ceases to be in business.

When it comes down to it, this story is the same no matter what business you're in. In the marketplace, your company is only as good as the eye-level trust it inspires in your customers. And internally, your organization is only as good as the eye-level trust that exists among its members. Consider how trust is earned and lost within the workplace. For example, a fundamental principle of management is establishing clear and defined objectives. When a person is new to a job, it's important to immediately set expectations so that he understands the rules of the game. Over time, as the employee meets or falls short of his agreements, trust in him is either built up or lost. Meanwhile, the new employee is assessing the situation from his perspective, looking at himself (*Can I do this job?*), his supervisor (*Will she help me to learn and treat me fairly?*), co-workers (*Will they support or undermine me?*), and the company as a whole (*Will this be an environment that allows me to grow and perform well?*). When those at the new workplace keep up their end of the bargain, the employee's trust in them—and the company—builds accordingly.

Eye-level trust within organizations can and should be maintained even when tough choices must be made, according to Santo ("Sandy") J. Costa. In the mid-to-late 1990s, Costa served as president and COO—and later, vice chairman—of Quintiles Transnational, an S&P 500 company that provides integrated product development and commercialization solutions to the pharmaceutical, biotechnology, and medical device industries. During Costa's tenure as president and COO, Quintiles grew from fewer than one thousand employees in eight countries to more than twenty thousand employees in thirty-one countries. "I've always viewed relationships in organizations as being covenantal and not contractual," says Costa. "A covenant is a shared commitment, and I think that you can only have shared commitments when you have trust." While Costa acknowledges that companies sometimes have to make hard decisions and take actions that may have negative effects on employees, this can be done in a way that nonetheless honors and respects those employees' trust. When a negative action is necessary, he says, *it shouldn't be taken in a way that seems haphazard, unjustified, or not clearly communicated. If you don't feel like you can take the time to let your people know what's going on in their lives within an organization, it shows you don't value them. And if people don't feel like they're valued, they certainly won't trust [you].[8]*

This is a lesson that one embattled company, Agilent Technologies, appears to have taken to heart.

Putting Trust to the Test: Agilent Technologies

Every year, *Fortune* lists its "100 Best Companies to Work For in America," based on an employee survey called the Great Place to Work Trust Index as well as an evaluation of company benefits and practices. Employees' opinions matter most, as their surveys count for two-thirds of a company's total score. In February 2002, *Fortune* featured a several-page spread on Agilent Technologies, which placed thirty-first among that year's honorees. The article talked glowingly about the "Agilent Way" and featured photos of smiling employees. The article's title? "How to Cut Pay, Lay Off 8,000 People, and Still Have Workers Who Love You."

"It may seem odd to award the Best Companies moniker to a company that laid off 8,000 people," *Fortune* conceded. However, the magazine went on to credit Agilent CEO Ned Barnholt with "driv[ing] his business forward through tough times without violating the workers' trust."[9] And times have been tough indeed for the Silicon Valley–based tech giant. As business soured in 2001, Agilent fought to avoid layoffs with cost-cutting measures and a temporary 10 percent pay cut across the board. It wasn't enough, however, and the company was forced to cut four thousand jobs at first, then four thousand more.

Fortune interviewed dozens of Agilent employees—both past and present—and found that nearly no one had a negative word to say. The company offered a generous severance package, but interviewees preferred to talk about the other ways Agilent handled the situation: "the Hail Mary steps the company took to avoid downsizing; the barrage of e-mails and face-to-face meetings with top management down; even the tired sound in the CEO's voice as he delivered news of mass layoffs."[10]

The magazine noted how Agilent, which was spun off by Hewlett-Packard in 1999, "considers itself the true keeper of the 'HP Way'—the management objectives devised by Hewlett and Packard that spelled out how to treat customers, shareholders, and most of all employees. The Way's key precept is that workers will give their best if they're treated honestly and listened to."[11] Barnholt made sure the Agilent Way was compatible with the demands of the market by also incorporating three new company values: focus, speed, and accountability.

These values have been put to the test. When Agilent needed to cut costs in 2001, it relied on the ingenuity of its employees instead of handing down directives. Agilent employees took the initiative, embracing cost cutting as a "calling." When the company temporarily cut salaries, employees cheered the move, understanding it might help save jobs. And finally, when layoffs were necessary, Agilent embarked on a downsizing campaign that was "two parts communication, one part execution." *Fortune* concluded, "Agilent had succeeded in turning the 'us vs. them' of corporate downsizing into just 'us.'"[12]

As of this writing, the jury is still out on Agilent. The downsizing has continued as the company struggles with losses; its workforce has now been reduced by approximately 30 percent from its peak in early 2001. Nevertheless, in an interview posted on the company's Web site, Ned Barnholt stressed his pride in how the people at Agilent have responded to the downturn: "Because they're staying the course, I'm confident that we'll come out of this difficult time a strong company."[13]

By the way, *Fortune* released its 2003 "Best Companies to Work For" list. Agilent was number thirty-three.

A Call to Action

Trust involves a dynamic give-and-take that is most evident at eye level: between a company and its customers, and within the company itself. It's at this level that we can understand trust as an actionable concept, one that is within our power. Eye-level trust is an asset that requires constant attention and vigilance—it requires that agreements be defined and kept, and accountability be understood and embraced. Because it demands this kind of participation from all those involved, eye-level trust truly enriches and solidifies relationships. And it's this kind of trust that the Accountable Organization seeks to achieve.

BUILDING THE
ACCOUNTABLE ORGANIZATION

1. Consider the level of trust in your own workplace.

   • Are senior managers trusted by others in the company? Do senior managers trust the "rank-and-file" employees? How would you characterize trust within your immediate work group and among different departments? What evidence do you have to support your position?

   • What do you consider to be barriers to building trust in the workplace? Why do these barriers exist?

   • What steps can you personally take to increase trust in your company?

2. Now consider the trust you have with customers.

   • Do you believe that your customers trust you? Do your customers trust your company more than your closest competitors? What evidence do you have to support your position?

   • Assume that trust is easily quantified. If you were to double the level of customer trust in your company, what impact would that have on sales?

   • Consider ideas that would double customer trust. Conversely, consider whether any of your company's current practices should be eliminated in order to enhance trust. What would it cost to implement such ideas? What price are you paying for not implementing these ideas?

CHAPTER TWO

ACCOUNTABILITY
Taking Responsibility for Choices

In the summer of 2002, we all watched as a succession of disgraced executives were led away in handcuffs, surrounded by FBI agents. For months, we heard about billions of investor dollars gone, thousands of jobs lost, and numerous individual retirements indefinitely postponed. Now the alleged bad guys were finally being called on the carpet, and the television cameras were there to capture it all.

Accountability As Guilt

If a picture is worth a thousand words, these images were orchestrated to emphasize only one: accountability. That is, accountability as guilt. Former Treasury Secretary Paul O'Neill was quoted as saying, "I think the people who have abused our trust, we ought to hang them from the very highest branches."[1]

It's no wonder that in the language of politics, accountability has the subtext of guilt. After all, these dramas are played out on the national stage, the numbers are staggering, and the alleged crimes of these wealthy individuals have made "victims" of the rest of us. It's not just that these people could afford to buy $15,000 umbrella stands for their Manhattan palaces or build $15 million mansions in Boca Raton. It's the American Dream to have the means to engage in such frivolity, if one so desires—but not by bilking hardworking investors and employees. "With each arrest, indictment and prosecution, we send this clear, unmistakable message: corrupt corporate executives are no better than common thieves when they betray their employees and steal from their investors," said Attorney General John Ashcroft at a press conference announcing the indictments of former WorldCom higher-ups. "Corporate executives who cheat investors, steal savings, and squander pensions will meet the judgment they fear and the punishment they deserve."[2]

Accountability as guilt may serve a purpose on the public stage. But what happens when we talk about accountability at eye level, in our own lives as individuals and in the roles we play at work? In speaking with several different executives, I found a range of perceptions on what it means to be "accountable":

"*I see accountability as simply being for any action that you take, there is someone who is holding you responsible for that action, or some series of people.*"

"*The foundation of accountability consists of measurable outcomes or expectations that you want to see happen, either in pure results or in approach and so on. Secondly, accountability is not the end of something, it's a part of everything you do . . . it's an ongoing process.*"

"*True accountability means* taking *responsibility. And I underline the word* taking *because I use it in the sense of accountability being actionable.*"

"*You're willing to stand up and declare your willingness to be in support of something—or you're willing to be the champion for something and take it forward. You can invite [accountability], but I don't think you can impose it on somebody . . . and if you believe you can, then I think you're setting up a situation for failure.*"[3]

While some of these responses focus on accountability as fulfilling the expectations of others, none of them describes it as designating who's at fault. And I believe that's important if we want to make eye-level accountability an integral—and welcomed—part of our everyday reality. Instead of focusing solely on assigning blame and punishment, there is a more constructive, healthier way to understand accountability—one that is crucial for building an Accountable Organization.

Who's Accountable Here?

Companies are nothing more than the collective efforts of people. And people aren't always willing to be accountable for their actions—particularly in times of discord. A story from my own company, FWI, illustrates how this can happen.

FWI has built a solid reputation for editorial integrity and excellence. Internally, the company is organized into three distinct areas: sales and marketing, administration, and editorial. As is common at many companies, there is an inherent tension between sales and production. Those in the editorial department are necessarily focused on the product: top-notch news pieces that are clear, accurate, and topical. Meanwhile, true to their mission, our account directors work tirelessly to land business—but sometimes landing so much business puts the rest of the company into overdrive.

It's important to point out that our culture is one that celebrates free time. I'm concerned that my employees keep reasonable hours, that they have a life outside of work. However, as is often the case at smaller, more entrepreneurial firms, it's also understood that when an urgent need arises, everyone needs to unite and pitch in.

Nevertheless, when a staff gets overwhelmed with work, preexisting conflict and tensions can be exacerbated. This is the situation we encountered a while back. For a two-week period, nearly every writer was out of the office, traveling to several medical conferences we were covering simultaneously. To handle the onslaught of work, virtually everyone involved with production was putting in eighteen-hour days. Office couches became makeshift beds. Unfortunately, and perhaps as a result of stress and frustration, there was a common perception among the writers and administrative staff that the salespeople weren't pulling their weight—that they were only interested in closing deals and didn't care how the product would actually be delivered.

Fed up, the writers went to their supervisor, the managing editor, to complain. She informed them, however, that there was little she could do and suggested that they write a group letter to *her* manager, the company's vice president and general manager. Meanwhile, he had already made it clear that this was a short-term problem and that everyone should stop complaining. Around this time, one of the writers came to me directly and asked me to intervene. The misery in the office was palpable. Later, after talking it through with the GM, we decided that the best course of action would be to have a companywide meeting and allow everyone to air their grievances so we could work toward a solution.

Soon afterward, we had our meeting. I chose my words carefully, knowing that what I said and how I said it would set the tone for what followed. I opened up the floor for discussion, encouraging everyone to speak their mind. I waited. I nudged and prodded. Abject silence. After more cajoling, I managed to pry loose a few comments, but no one was willing to go out on a limb.

I left the meeting totally dejected. Given the opportunity to take a stand, to lay their concerns on the line, no one was willing to claim ownership of his or her role in the situation. We were all looking for someone to blame. The writers blamed the GM for overworking them and not being sensitive to their concerns. The managing editor relinquished her responsibility, placing blame on the GM and the sales organization. Coming from a sales background, the GM didn't fully understand the writers' perspective and had little empathy. And I wasn't without fault. After all, I was the CEO. The buck stops with me, right?

About a week after our meeting, we instituted several policy changes that would help address work spikes in the future. But I wasn't worried about minor pragmatic fixes. What concerned me more was that in this situation, we—as individuals and as a collective—had willingly relinquished accountability. And it would take more than a new paragraph in the procedure manual to repair that.

Accountability As Ownership

Achieving eye-level accountability is an ongoing process, one that includes struggles, setbacks, and the occasional fall off the wagon. From its inception, FWI was supposed to embody my vision of an Accountable Organization. But being a human endeavor, it sometimes misses the mark—and there are no quick and easy remedies.

More important, placing eye-level accountability in the context of blame leads to injured relationships and, ultimately, loss of trust. Perhaps we have been conditioned by our litigious society to associate accountability with liability, to believe that the risk of unpleasantness and cost outweighs the potential for understanding and reward. Because of this perception, often-times we view accountability as a burden—and what's worse, a burden that is thrust upon us without our permission.

Think for a moment about the things in life for which you're on the hook, the things you absolutely have to do. If you were to write those things down, what would be on your list? Eating, sleeping, taking care of children (and/or parents and/or pets), working, paying taxes, exercising, doing the laundry, cleaning the house, mowing the grass?

Now consider those things that you *choose* to do. For a lot of the things we do, the difference between "have to" and "choose to" is a matter of obligation versus recreation. We often associate our "choose-tos" with free time—they're how we recharge our batteries: hiking, swimming, reading, listen-ing to music, playing golf, and so on. Predictably, some things show up on both lists: children, while they represent an awe-some, never-ending responsibility, are also likely number one on parents' choose-to lists.[4]

If you were to compare your lists, which one would be longer? If it's the "have-to" list, you're not alone—after all, it's the American way. We're a nation of doers; we wear busyness as a badge of honor. Over time, however, that busyness can feed upon itself, until finally we feel as if we're on the hook for *everything*. But the truth is—and as trite as it may sound—we always have a choice, even when it comes to those things in our lives that seem inconceivable *not* to do. Of course, our choices come with sometimes painful consequences, but the bottom line is that we are the ones who ultimately make the decision.

In short, accountability means owning and accepting responsibility for the choices we make in life. We often disavow this ownership position, and instead relegate large portions of our lives to the have-to column. We *have* to do such-and-such. There's no choice in the matter. And thus we willingly give over the controls to some perceived larger force, not realizing the price we ultimately pay—or realizing only too late, after we find ourselves in crisis.

The price we pay for denying accountability is loss of power and trust. When we give up ownership, we become frustrated, resentful, angry. We find refuge in cynicism and indulge in blame—not exactly the best position for being completely answerable for agreements, be they implied or explicit. After all, if the buck doesn't stop with us when it comes to the choices we make for ourselves, how can we truly be accountable when it comes to our relationships with others?

John Kadlic is vice president, client services, for Blue Diesel—an Ohio-based interactive agency. He knows where the buck stops. He manages a team of account executives and is ultimately responsible for the company's book of business. John expects nothing less than full accountability from his team, which he describes as follows:

> *Are you the one who's responsible for doing what you say? Do you deliver on what you commit to people what you will do, whether they're external or internal? And when*

you fall down, do you own up to that? And when you're
successful, do you take that praise professionally and
acknowledge the others that contributed to your success?[5]

Stakeholders, Not Placeholders:
The Accountable Organization

On my way home from a business trip, I struck up a conversation with a ticket agent. We got on the topic of some
recent unpopular decisions the airline had made concerning seating and ticketing. I was giving the agent my thoughts
on the matter—I wasn't happy about these moves, and she
wasn't surprised.

"The thing is," she said, "they never even asked us about
what we thought about the policy. We're the ones on the front
lines, the ones dealing with weary travelers every day. In all my
years, I've never been asked about my opinion about anything."
She continued, "It's my job to take care of customers. But every
time they pull something like this it limits my ability to do what
they pay me to do: keep you flying our airline and not someone
else's. I'm just a number; I do what they tell me. I suppose that's
what it's like working for any large company."

Despite her enormous influence on the customer experience, the ticket agent's opinion was never solicited by the organization's leadership—or even, for that matter, the marketing
unit. Her attitude toward upper management was "us versus
them." She felt undervalued and replaceable. While she

believed that she played an important role as an ambassador for the company, within the company she felt insignificant, invisible. She felt powerless to effect any change whatsoever.

Nonetheless, the ticket agent—who had a long tenure with the airline—made it clear that she loved her company and wanted to see it do better by its employees and customers. She pleaded with me to write the airline and protest some of its new policies: "As a loyal customer, maybe they'll listen to you." I had actually had a similar conversation about six months before with a different gate agent about yet another of the airline's unpopular edicts.

Based on what the gate agents told me, I understood that they wanted to create for their customers the best possible experience of this airline—and because of their position on the front lines, they were uniquely positioned to do so. They wanted to be proud of the product they were delivering. They wanted to be a factor in the airline's success. But they felt they could only contribute within defined parameters: carrying out company policy as dictated from above. (The airline I'm referring to isn't Southwest. As we will see in chapter 10, I likely would have had a very different conversation with a Southwest ticket agent.)

Yes, it was sad that these gate agents felt they had to resort to recruiting customers to take up their causes—not only because of what it said about their company's accountability, but also what it said about their own. True, the ticket agents might have felt they had no other recourse than to complain to customers, but was this the best way to effect change? Or should they have tried harder to find more appropriate ways to help the airline right itself? For that is what it means to be part of building an Accountable Organization: being an active stakeholder, not a passive placeholder. Being a true stakeholder doesn't mean just being a beneficiary—it requires action, stepping forward, and claiming one's responsibility as well as one's due. For if ownership of our choices and actions is the hallmark of personal accountability, it is also key to being a true stakeholder in a company. And in Accountable Organizations, meaningful ownership and responsibility is both facilitated by management *and* sought by employees.

Accountability: Integral to Integrity

Architects of Accountable Organizations find that a crucial part of their job is training people to be stakeholders: educating them to embrace ownership on both an individual level and an organizational level. For true stakeholders understand how their choices impact not only themselves, but also the wider organization. They understand and embrace their role in upholding the true bedrock of Accountable Organizations: *integrity.*

BUILDING THE
ACCOUNTABLE ORGANIZATION

1. Does your definition of accountability differ from the one proposed in this book, and if so, how?

2. Think about the concept of accountability as it is currently practiced in your organization. Can you identify aspects of your organization's environment or policies that discourage a culture of ownership? On the flip side, which aspects encourage accountability?

3. Think about how you personally practice accountability within your organization. Can you think of a difficult situation in which you deflected ownership of your role? Consider whether the outcome would have differed had you been fully accountable.

4. Consider how you influence others' accountability in their relationships with you. Do you engage in the "blame game" with others? If so, what changes can you make to change your—and their—perspectives?

CHAPTER THREE

INTEGRITY
Doing the Right Thing

A magazine ad for Charles Schwab features a middle-aged man named John—an individual investor, a regular guy. According to John, he moved his money to the discount brokerage because "before, I very rarely heard a sell recommendation. I feel that Schwab has my interests at heart."[1]

"Let's Put Some Lipstick on This Pig"

In summer 2002, Schwab rolled out a television commercial that took dead aim at its full-service rivals. The ad portrayed a smarmy Wall Street sales manager urging his brokers to push a junk stock to clients.

Sales manager: Tell your customers it's red hot. This one is *en fuego.* Just don't mention the fundamentals; they stink. Let's put some lipstick on this pig. Get to work, people.

Voiceover: There's never been a better time for Charles Schwab.[2]

The commercial aired just weeks after Merrill Lynch agreed to pay $100 million to settle allegations that the company's investment advice was tainted by conflicts of interest. The investigation, led by New York State Attorney General Eliot Spitzer, brought to light e-mails in which Merrill analysts ridiculed Internet companies they were publicly recommending—companies that were important to Merrill's banking business. Thus, the timing of Schwab's commercial was particularly sharp (too sharp for CBS, which declined to air it). Indeed, Schwab seemed to capitalize on people's disgust with the coziness between analysts and investment bankers on Wall Street: according to the firm, individual investors shifted $30 billion into accounts there in 2002.

Then, the end of the year brought news of a global settlement with the securities industry that dwarfed the earlier Merrill Lynch agreement. Spitzer, the SEC, the NYSE, and other regulators announced in late December that ten of the nation's top investment firms had agreed to pay $1.4 billion to make amends for conflicts of interest regarding stock research.[3] Among other terms, the firms also agreed to sever the links between research and investment banking, including analysts' pay.

Predictably, the announcement was applauded by some and scoffed at by others. However, no matter the ultimate verdict on the effectiveness of the settlement or even its righteousness, the line at the time was that something had to be done, finally, in the name of one thing: integrity. "This agreement will permanently change the way Wall Street operates," declared Spitzer in a press release. "Our objective throughout the investigation and negotiations has been to protect the small investor and restore integrity to the marketplace." Robert Glauber, chairman and CEO of the National Association of Securities Dealers, was quoted as saying the settlement "demonstrates NASD's determination to investigate and sanction practices that harm investors and the integrity of the markets." And Dick Grasso, then NYSE chairman and CEO, added, "Investors need to know that the firms they do business with act only with the highest standards of honesty and integrity, putting investors' interests ahead of all others."[4]

Integrity Defined

Integrity. It's something to protect, something to fight for. And as the floodwaters of scandal kept rising, the word itself became a lifeline for politicians and business leaders scrambling to reach higher ground. There's a certain magic about it, as Yale law professor Stephen L. Carter relates in his 1996 book, *Integrity:*

> *A couple of years ago I began a university commencement address by telling the audience that I was going to*

talk about integrity. The crowd broke into applause. Applause! Just because they had heard the word integrity—that's how starved for it they were. They had no idea how I was using the word, or what I was going to say about it, or, indeed, whether I was for it or against it. But they knew they liked the idea of simply talking about it. This celebration of integrity is intriguing: we seem to carry on a passionate love affair with a word that we scarcely pause to define.[5]

The word *integrity* just *sounds* good. It's one of those words that inspire general impressions of virtue and substance. As Carter says, "Integrity is that stuff we always say we want more of."[6] But how can we truly understand integrity at eye level, as an actionable concept? One person I spoke to said integrity means "what I show and what I feel are congruent." Another described it as "being honest with yourself and others." Magill's *Ethics* defines integrity as "consistent adherence to moral, intellectual, professional, or artistic principles despite temptation to abandon them."[7] For me, integrity begins with the alignment of beliefs and actions, the correspondence of values and volition. It implies completeness and solidity—for example, we often use the word to refer to the physical soundness of a structure. When people have integrity, who they are and what they do are not divided. They are whole.

I'm sure you know people with integrity. It's likely you admire or respect them, and it's not hard to see why: these people stick to their convictions, even if it costs them personally.

But there's more to it, for integrity can't exist in a moral vacuum. If integrity simply meant sticking to one's convictions, one could claim, for example, that bigoted people who commit hate crimes have integrity. No, to have integrity, one's actions must express values that are founded on the Golden Rule—the bedrock morality of "doing unto others"—from which we get the compassion and intuitive sense of justice that define us as decent human beings. People who truly have integrity not only stick to their convictions, they do what's *right*.

Integrity's Place in a Country Where Winning Is Everything

Sure, you might say. We try to live by the Golden Rule when it comes to our personal relationships. But when it comes to business, to professional achievement, the Golden Rule often-times morphs into something more mercenary: "Beat the competition at any cost; they'd do the same to you." In this country, competition and winning are our great traditions. Winning, however, has come to be measured solely as having *more*—and nine times out of ten, we're talking about money. Money is one of the most objective, unambiguous measuring sticks we have for success. And as an entrepreneur, I'm aware of the fact that, whatever else its aims, a company is ultimately in business to make money. It has to be, not only to grow, but merely to survive.

So, does integrity have a place in today's business environment? After all, during the roaring nineties no one complained about aggressive companies; a rising tide lifts all boats, so we were content not to ask how their phenomenal "growth" was being achieved. Recalling the words of Alan Greenspan, our irrational exuberance gave way to infectious greed. It was the eighties all over again, except this time greed's mechanism was the Information Economy and the power of the Internet. We became addicted to money—though some would say we always have been—and one of the hallmarks of addiction is a focus on the immediate payoff, even when the result is long-term disaster.

However, while greed may seem to have tainted the quintessential American values of competition and winning, integrity can bring them back into the light. Sandy Costa, now in private law practice, tells a story of integrity in a competitor:

I had a tough negotiation involving a property matter. It was worth millions of dollars. This lawyer was representing a builder, I was representing one of the companies I work for.

Well, one of our assistants hit a wrong button on the fax machine and accidentally faxed this lawyer a crucial document that we had written internally. So I called him and explained the situation. He put the phone down, walked to the fax machine, sat back down, and said, "I am now tearing it up." And I heard him ripping paper.

To this day, there's no question in my mind that he tore that document up. That's because I had dealt with this person long enough and I was absolutely certain of his integrity. This is the type of person you love to deal with, as opposed to the one who would be running down the hall saying, "Guess what I just got!"

At the end of the day, if you're dealing with someone in any relationship that is at some level contentious—and I don't mean that in a pejorative sense—and yet you find him easy to deal with, it's probably because that person has integrity.[8]

Integrity is not incompatible with competition, with seeking to win and earn a profit. Honest competition brings out the best in us, and profits ensure that an organization endures and is able to impact people's lives, be they customers, investors, or employees.

Can We Legislate Integrity?

Understandably, the corporate scandals led to an outcry for action. Wrongdoing should not go unpunished. But as a broader issue, can we rely on legislation—or litigation—to restore integrity to business? After all, the Sarbanes-Oxley Act was designed to do just that. Among other provisions, it created a regulatory board to oversee the accounting industry. Auditing firms would no longer be allowed to provide consulting services that create conflicts of interest. Whistle-blowers would receive greater protection, and executives who deliberately defrauded investors would face long prison terms.

While Sarbanes-Oxley was passed to create systems for corporate accountability, it is also an attempt to legislate business ethics. (As noted earlier, the law requires that companies have a formal code of ethics policy for their executive teams.) But again, it raises the question: Aside from protecting us from the real crooks, can we rely on law to stand in for integrity? Or, should we instead make defending integrity the responsibility of us all, regardless of whether we lead a company or are a member of its rank and file?

This question is currently being debated in the academic realm, as colleges and universities are struggling to combat a steady rise in cheating. According to a 1999 survey conducted at twenty-one campuses by Dr. Donald McCabe, founding president of the Center for Academic Integrity, over 75 percent of participating students admitted to some form of cheating. Approximately one-third confessed to cheating on tests, while half admitted to cheating on written assignments. CAI noted that Internet plagiarism is a particular problem: in a 2001 survey, 41 percent of participating students admitted to lifting material from the Internet and using it in papers without proper citation. What's more, 68 percent of students felt this sort of behavior was "not a serious issue."[9]

I received my undergraduate degree from Knox College, a small liberal arts school in Galesburg, Illinois. The college is proud of its "honor system," which was introduced through student initiative in 1951. Under this system, Knox faculty members do not proctor exams; students may take tests in any public space in the building. Cases of alleged academic dishonesty are heard by an "honor board" made up of students and faculty advisors. Penalties may vary, but usually mean an F in the course for a first offense and expulsion for a second offense.

The honor system operates with the understanding that each student "is morally responsible for the integrity of his or her own work." Similarly, students are "morally obligated to take action if a violation is seen." Failure to report cheating to the honor board is not in itself a violation, but students who witness cheating are expected to "handle the situation in ways consistent with their conscience and the integrity of the academic community."[10]

Note the use of the word *community*. In placing the responsibility for integrity squarely on the shoulders of its students, the college emphasizes the communal nature of education and the importance of trust among those taking part in it. There is guardianship via the honor board and its power to impose penalties, but the overarching message is one of ownership: individual students are accountable for the education they receive. Together, they are accountable for creating the kind of community that supports the highest intellectual standards. If they fall short on this responsibility, other members of the community will take them to task.

Some would claim that honor codes are naïve. In fact, many institutions have begun implementing electronic anti-cheating measures as a deterrent. One company, Turnitin.com, offers a plagiarism prevention system that compares submitted papers against Internet content. Turnitin.com has thousands of high schools and universities as clients; the site boasts that it "presently protects more than 5,000,000 students in over 50 countries."[11] It's an interesting word choice: *protects*. Granted, the ease of information available on the Internet may confuse the issue of plagiarism for students. However, by its very nature, this kind of policing doesn't reinforce a sense of trust and community as an honor code does. If a mechanism such as Turnitin.com is in place to protect students from plagiarism, then it necessarily takes some of the ownership away from them.

Perhaps it's unrealistic to think that communities of students can be expected to take full responsibility for the integrity of their education. However, surveys conducted by CAI among students at forty-eight campuses show that the level of test cheating at institutions with honor codes is generally one-third to one-half lower than that at schools without codes. The level of cheating on written assignments at schools with honor codes is lower by one-fourth to one-third.[12] Furthermore, teachers and students achieve more of a reciprocal trust and respect. CAI offers the following testimony from a student:

> *This semester a professor excused me from taking a test at the normal time and allowed me to choose the time and date when I could make it up. Mutual trust was built from day one of this semester and has influenced the way I approach the course. I feel an obligation to my teacher to perform to the best of my ability, which I credit to the respect we have for one another in our different roles.*[13]

I make the point strongly about the college environment because today's students are the business leaders of tomorrow. What rules they learn about integrity, accountability, and trust are brought with them into the workplace. On the other hand, is it naïve to think that communities of businesspeople, if expected to take full responsibility for the integrity of their workplace, will embrace the opportunity? Is it naïve to think that they can create the same kind of reciprocal trust and respect? Perhaps there is hope that if we embrace our responsibility for contributing to the integrity of our workplaces—if we care enough to figure out what is the right thing to do— then we'll help create workplaces built on trust. Then we'll help create Accountable Organizations.

So, What Does It Take to Operate with Integrity?

Earlier in this chapter, I noted how it's no surprise that we are drawn to people with integrity, that we place our trust in them. Similarly, companies that operate with integrity are admired and trusted. They have the loyalty of their customers, employees, and other stakeholders. But how do these individuals and organizations get this way? What does operating with integrity entail?

My first lesson in this came soon after I started FWI. We had been in business for about six months and were struggling, really struggling, to keep our doors open. We had $3,000 in our bank account, with virtually no resources upon which to draw. Personally, I was almost three months late on my home mortgage, having thrown every bit of money I had at the business. I had already borrowed emergency funds from friends and family to tide me over. In short, I had sunk about as low as I could go. I envisioned my former colleagues laughing at me: *We told you so. We knew you'd never make it on your own.*

About that time my wife left the country to attend her grandfather's funeral. The bedrock of my life was inaccessible, even by phone. I was depressed and lonely. It was New Year's Eve, 1994, and I sat alone in my house, watching *It's a Wonderful Life* and largely missing the point of the movie.

Then, a miracle happened. A few days later, one of my old bosses—a close friend and mentor—called with a project. The awful feeling of despair, the weight I had felt on my back, was suddenly gone.

I was ecstatic . . . that is, until my friend began to describe the project. As he spoke, I realized very quickly that I didn't have the resources or experience to deliver what he was asking. Not a chance. My stomach resumed its churning as I went ahead anyway and told him, "Sure, I'll have the project completed by the end of next week."

The following week was one of the worst I've ever experienced. I worked day and night, forgoing sleep and food, pursuing a lost cause. When the deadline came and I presented my work, I knew that I had failed. What was worse, I knew I should never have taken the project in the first place, that I had misrepresented what I could do. Now my friend was two weeks behind schedule and needed to find another vendor to do the job properly.

I didn't even bother asking for money, and he didn't bother to offer any. It would be two years before I could face my friend again and begin to repair the damage I'd done.

Yes, this was a lesson in honesty. I should have been honest with my friend and told him up front that I would have to take a pass. But more important, it was a lesson in integrity. I was down and out, and I made a decision based on what was expedient, not what was right. I compromised my values by taking a project I couldn't possibly handle—thus guaranteeing that the work I produced would disappoint my client. The price I paid was damage to my friend's trust in me, damage that would require much time and effort to repair.

After this experience, I never again accepted a job we couldn't handle, no matter how badly we needed the money. I learned that while maintaining my integrity in the face of financial adversity would be difficult, it would be much more difficult to repair the long-term damage done to my relationships, both business and personal.

This first lesson in integrity would be followed by countless others. Over time, through my experience with FWI, I've found that there are a few basic components to operating with integrity, both on an individual level and as an Accountable Organization. First of all, we must be clear about our values and beliefs and be honest about their rightness, that is, how they measure up morally. Similarly, a company must have the same clarity about its vision and mission. In short, we have to determine the kind of people we want to be and organizations we want to create. Without this understanding, there is no standard against which to evaluate our actions.

Integrity is achieved when we act in alignment with our values and beliefs, and when a company acts in accordance with its vision and mission. Otherwise, these intentions don't count for much—they remain untested and unproven. Acting in alignment doesn't happen by chance, however; it requires conscious decisions (and in organizations, the conscious decisions of many). In this way, accountability is how we express our integrity as individuals and as companies: we take full responsibility for the rightness of our choices, as well as for their consequences.

Finally, we must aim for continuity. Day in, day out we make choices both large and small in relation to ourselves and our families, friends, and colleagues—anyone and everyone with whom we come in contact. Every day, companies are also making myriad decisions that impact their stakeholders to varying degrees. As such, integrity is at issue from moment to moment, not just when we're faced with fork-in-the-road challenges. Living and operating with integrity are continuing commitments. We can gauge our success as a running total: the major tests we face obviously move the balance one way or the other, but it's those little decisions that quietly add up.

Values in Action

Trust, accountability, integrity . . . As we've seen in the preceding chapters, these are heady topics. So many companies claim these as core values, but that's the easy part. The hard part comes in actually trying to express these values in action, in pulling them down from the ether and giving them life at eye level. Agilent was successful in doing this; as *Fortune* pointed out, the company earned its employees' trust when times were good, so it had a "head start" in maintaining that trust when its fortunes turned.[14]

Among the thousands upon thousands of American companies, Enron and the like are outliers. The vast majority of companies are led and staffed by honorable people who want to do well financially, but do so ethically. They want their work to mean something. They want to create something they can be proud of. In short, they want to build Accountable Organizations of their own. And to build anything, one needs tools.

BUILDING THE ACCOUNTABLE ORGANIZATION

1. Is your organizational culture one that emphasizes integrity as much as winning? How does this affect morale and productivity? What kind of role, if any, does your organization's leadership take in promoting integrity?

2. Are there standard business practices within your industry that create ethical dilemmas and challenges to integrity? If your company were to challenge those institutionalized practices, what would be the outcome?

3. What was the last dilemma you faced that challenged your personal integrity? Are you comfortable with how you resolved the dilemma? In retrospect, is there anything you would have done differently?

4. Recall Sandy Costa's story about dealing with a competitor who had integrity. Does your perception of other people's integrity influence how you interact with them, and if so, why? If you believe someone is not acting with integrity, do you feel it gives you license to do the same?

CHAPTER FOUR

PURPOSE
Clarifying What You Stand For

In the movie *Jerry Maguire,* successful sports agent Jerry Maguire seems to have it all: money, a nice house and car, a beautiful fiancée. But he's conflicted. He senses that the business of sports representation is going in the wrong direction—that *he* is going in the wrong direction. One night while at a conference in Miami, Jerry sits down at his laptop and starts writing. And writing. In a burst of inspiration, he outlines what the business *should* be about: fewer clients, not more. Less quantity, more quality. A focus on people, not money.

At first, Jerry's sure he'll just delete his manifesto and go back to bed. Instead, he ends up going to a twenty-four-hour copy center and distributing his masterpiece to everyone at the conference before daybreak. Needless to say, given the cynicism of his business, Jerry's mission statement isn't welcomed, and he promptly loses his job. He struggles to make a new start with the one employee and the one client who believe in him. And in the end, he finds much more meaningful—and promising—success than he ever had before.

Of course, *Jerry Maguire* is a Hollywood fable: the happy ending is written into the script long before the opening credits roll. Real life doesn't come with such guarantees. But part of the reason audiences connect with the movie is our desire for clarity. We identify with Jerry's middle-of-the-night epiphany—and admire his recklessness in actually letting that epiphany see the light of day.

Most of us have an understanding of our fundamental beliefs of right and wrong. But far fewer of us have taken the time to clearly define the principles by which we will live and the goals we want to achieve. It's more than just a worthwhile exercise; it's necessary for making sure that our lives are governed by what we believe in, not just by what's expedient. The same is true for companies. If expediency is allowed to rule, an organization doesn't control its course. Instead, decisions are made in the service of short-term considerations rather than long-term success.

The Importance of Clarity

I still have "the napkin," that piece of paper on which I first jotted down the idea that would become FaxWatch, Inc. I was twenty-seven years old at the time, in the company of a good friend, having a cold beer. I sketched out with broad strokes what I dreamed was possible in a company—what I knew was possible. I had been truly inspired, as was my friend, who would commit his time and energy to helping me get the company off the ground. Several years later, however, I found myself searching for that inspiration. I had lost the zeal, the sense of mission that once had moved me.

Those years had been successful, to be sure. After weathering some early challenges, FaxWatch started growing and didn't stop. We had to find larger and larger offices. The company consistently turned a profit and stayed out of debt, all without the help of outside investors. We were proud to be named twice to the *Inc.* 500 list of America's fastest-growing private companies.

But despite all this, I found myself missing the forest for the trees. I had thrown myself heart and soul into making FaxWatch a success, and indeed it was. But in working frenetically to grow the company, I lost sight of why I started it in the first place. I let myself become consumed, forgetting to take care of my relationships and my health, both mental and physical. It's a trap that many entrepreneurs fall into—instead of running the business, I was letting it run me. About that time I'd begun reading Michael Gerber's infamous manifesto on entrepreneurship, *The E-Myth Revisited.* His words hit home:

> *You're* consumed *by the business and the possibility of losing it. And so you put everything you have into it. And, for whatever reason, you manage to keep it going. Day after*

*day, fighting the same battles, in exactly the same way you
did before. You never change. Night after night, you go
home to unwind, only to wind up tighter in anticipation
of tomorrow.... You're like a twelve-cylinder engine working on one cylinder, pumping away, trying with everything
you've got to produce twelve cylinders' worth of results. But
finally, and inevitably, there's nothing left.... Something
has to give, and that something is you.*[1]

Realizing that something had to change, I took stock of my
life. I did a lot of writing and reflecting; I read voraciously,
enlisting the help of a wide variety of authors and thinkers; I
attended seminars and workshops. Again and again, one word
continued to surface: *integrity*—the alignment of beliefs and
actions, anchored in what's right.

So I looked beyond the choices I was making and examined what it was I wanted to stand for. It was hard and often-
times frustrating work. However, once I defined my core
principles, I then had a meaningful measuring stick against
which to compare my choices. From this position of understanding and ownership, I began to make amends for the relationships I'd damaged. I could become truly accountable and
honor the trust of the important people in my life. I committed fully to a new way of doing things.

Perhaps it was coincidence, but this personal process happened to dovetail with a change at FaxWatch. As we entered a
new century, I was faced with a dilemma: our archaic company
name. When I started the company in 1994, e-mail as we know

it was still in its infancy. We delivered our publications to readers' desktops by fax—hence the name, FaxWatch.

As our reputation for quality spread, "FaxWatch" became synonymous with our information services. Even though each of our publications has its own title, readers would talk about starting their workday with "my FaxWatch." Furthermore, we had developed name recognition among the corporations with whom we partnered. It's the kind of brand equity that advertising dollars can't buy. The problem was that the name FaxWatch in and of itself was in danger of becoming something of a liability as well.

The Internet had changed how people wanted to receive information. Despite the fact that customers recognized the FaxWatch name and associated it with timely, high-quality information, they also associated it with fax delivery. While we expanded our services to include content for corporate intranets and e-newsletters, customers didn't think to call us because these capabilities weren't part of our name.

So, in the fall of 2001, I hired a branding agency to help reposition FaxWatch. With the help of my employees, we ended up with hundreds of potential new names. I'll admit that the naming process became something of an obsession for me; I thought I could find that one perfect name, that one word or phrase that would encompass all the different aspects of our business. I finally narrowed the list down to ten, including such candidates as Triple Helix and Stratamedica. I wasn't satisfied. I was on a quest for the Holy Grail of corporate monikers, the be-all and end-all.

And then something interesting happened. I discovered that developing a new "image" for our company went beyond choosing the ultimate name or the coolest logo. Much like my own personal process, it meant going deeper and examining just what we wanted to stand for going forward. It meant achieving clarity. I looked around at my company and realized that we were at a critical juncture, just like I myself had been a short time before.

Like all companies, we had encountered tests of integrity since the day we opened our doors. In the early days, we faced these tests as the small, tight unit we were. But now, as I looked around and counted an ever-growing number of faces, I worried about how to pass along those principles, how to make them live in a company that was rapidly becoming not so small. Indeed, it was even a question of how well everyone in the company, even at our current size, truly understood what it was all about.

So the process of "rebranding" was truly an education, both for me and for my employees. Our branding agency interviewed people both inside the company and out: production staff, writers, salespeople, customers. No leading questions, just an honest analysis of how they perceived what we did, how we did it, and why. Armed with the results, we were able to identify areas of confusion among customers and make a clear statement about who we are.

And our name? Turns out the answer had been in front of me all along. Even though "FaxWatch, Inc." reflected our pre-Internet beginnings, that alone wasn't worth throwing away so much hard-won brand equity—or, on a more personal level, for losing the history behind the name. So we chose a new identity that built on that heritage while bringing our company into the twenty-first century. We introduced our new name—FWI—emblazoned on a fiery red logo, confident and clear about what stood behind it.

The Power of Values and Purpose

The guiding principles of mission, vision, and values have been written about time and again, and with good reason. They provide members of an organization with context:

Mission: What your organization is doing and why (framed in relation to the customer)

Vision: Where you are going (aspirational and motivational)

Values: The rules you play by (what you stand for)

Many people believe a company can define its guiding principles by consensus. While I believe it is absolutely necessary to get input from employees and customers, ultimately this task must be the responsibility of the CEO. I've learned this through experience: previous efforts involving the whole company—while valuable—just hadn't articulated the kind of concrete direction that FWI needed. So, I isolated myself for twenty-four hours and examined what I wanted FWI to be ... what I wanted it to stand for. I looked back at where we had been as a company: our successes, our failures, our products, our people. I thought about where we were today and where I'd like us to go tomorrow.

I considered each question from three standpoints: my personal feelings and aspirations for the company; our customers' point of view, obtained through focus groups and years of meetings; and, just as important, the opinions of my employees, both past and present. In taking these different perspectives into consideration, I tried my best to ensure that the direction I defined for FWI would be clearly and consistently understood by all its stakeholders.

My first conclusion was that values came before all else. It only makes sense—you can't truly be accountable and earn trust without first gaining a sense of your own values. Similarly, it's an empty exercise to develop statements of vision and mission if you first don't understand your company's core values. In *Good to Great*, Jim Collins writes,

> *An important caveat to the concept of core values is that there are no specific "right" core values for becoming an enduring great company. ... A company need not have passion for its customers (Sony didn't), or respect for the individual (Disney didn't), or quality (Wal-Mart didn't), or social responsibility (Ford didn't) in order to become enduring and great. The point is not what core values you have, but that you have core values at all, that you know what they are, that you build them*

explicitly into the organization, and that you preserve
them over time.²

Should values be aspirational? Yes. But while they should
represent your highest ideals, they also must represent your true
beliefs, not just a laundry list of every noble principle you can
think of. It is difficult, if not impossible, to be truly guided by
a statement of values in which you are not personally invested.

FWI Values

Several years before, we as a company had collectively developed a long list of values to which we aspired. This list included
entries such as these: be the best, make a difference, be focused,
have fun, and so on. On the surface, there was nothing wrong
with this list. Yet I felt compelled to revisit and revise it. Why?
First of all, while I don't believe that employees should have to
memorize each and every word of a values statement, the values themselves should be brief and memorable. I felt this list
was too long and disconnected. Secondly, it was obvious that
some of the entries were more cultural descriptors rather than
significant guiding principles, which pass the litmus test of
"What do we stand for?" For example, while it's an important
aspect of our company culture, do we really "stand for" having fun?

Finally, even though "be the best," "make a difference," "be
focused," and "embrace change" didn't make the final list, that
doesn't mean we don't strive for excellence and innovation.
However, I felt the bedrock values that underlie the relationships

---

FWI VALUES STATEMENT

At FWI, our values guide how we work and how we care for our customers and colleagues.

- **Integrity.** Integrity is the foundation of FWI: it's what distinguishes our products, our relationships with customers, and our commitments to each other. We strive to do what's right—even when it's not popular to do so.

- **Accountability.** We take responsibility for our actions. We honor our commitments, understanding that a promise made is a promise guaranteed.

- **Trust.** We seek to create healthy, sustained relationships based on trust. We create trust through open communication, treating people with respect, and living up to our values of integrity and accountability.

---

both within and outside FWI were first and foremost. In fact, as addressed later, organizational excellence and innovation are the result of a company's dedication to the values that strengthen and sustain stakeholder relationships. So, in the end, I found that I needed to look no further than the values of integrity, accountability, and trust.

Ultimately, the FWI values statement is a constant reminder for all of us at the company. All the stakeholders know what our values are and what they mean. These values guide how we work, the decisions we make, and most important, how we treat each other and our customers. By keeping the list to its essential components—no matter what yours may be—you create a values statement that is memorable and lasting.

After values come an organization's mission and vision: its daily business and its ultimate goal. "People joined within a company can be inspired by shared values," writes brand strategy consultant Daryl Travis. "But they can also be motivated by shared purpose. And the two are not the same. Values relate to ideals and principles. Purpose relates to strategy and action."[3] The debate continues about whether to separate mission from vision; for me, the answer emerged from my own defining process. While there was a distinction between our day-to-day business and what we ultimately dreamed of becoming, I found the two were so interconnected that it made the most sense to combine them into one "purpose statement." A purpose combines the mission and vision into one statement that brings a sense of the aspirational to the everyday. It reminds stakeholders about the meaning behind their jobs— and helps frame their daily decision making within the context of a larger companywide goal.

A visionary statement leads off our purpose. In an earlier team visioning exercise, at FWI we had focused on the impact of what we do: by providing the highest quality unbiased news and information to our readers, we are indeed enhancing health care. So, when it came to formulating our purpose statement, I placed that "ultimate impact" component front and center. We leverage the power of information to enhance *human health.* By infusing our daily mission with our larger aspiration, that one sentence reframed and transformed the

---

FWI PURPOSE STATEMENT

At FWI, we leverage the power of information to enhance human health.

The FWI brand is a symbol of integrity, authority, and trust. Through unequaled information products and services, our purpose is to

- Provide industry executives with tools to be effective, productive, and influential—assisting them to be exceptional managers and leaders
- Inform health care providers of innovations in medicine and health care delivery—helping them to provide better care for their patients
- Educate consumers and patients—empowering them to be more in control of their health care

---

importance of our work for everyone in the company. Our purpose is indeed larger than the research, writing, and editing we do on a daily basis—but it's through these day-to-day activities that we get there.

Next, I wanted to reinforce what our brand stood for: integrity (of the information itself, as well as how we interact with our customers); authority (the earned right to be experts in health care); and trust (that our readers can trust our judgment in what we report and how we report it). Finally, our purpose needed to be in the present, actionable, and framed by what we do for our different customers and how we impact their lives. This last point bears repeating: your purpose statement serves no purpose if it doesn't describe what you do for your customers.

As important as it is for leaders to define their organization's values and purpose, communicating these principles and goals in a meaningful way is even more critical. After I presented FWI's values and purpose, I gave my employees free rein to critique what they saw. I specifically asked them what they felt was missing and, conversely, what they felt was out of place. I wanted to get their perspective on whether the statements were challenging or unrealistic. Armed with this feedback, I went back and finalized our values and purpose statements. The ultimate decision was mine, but by seeking the input of my employees, I went a long way toward creating buy-in.

After previous well-meaning attempts, this final approach to identifying our values and purpose proved definitive. As FWI's leader, I drove the process and made the final call. The values came first before all else, because, I believe, a company's values are more important than any product it makes. The language is actionable, inspirational, and meaningful to everyone in the organization, be they a veteran or a new hire. And most important, the story is unique to our company—the values and purpose relate what we stand for, who we are, and what we aspire to be.

Can an organization's values and purpose change over time? Conventional wisdom suggests that values should be immutable—that long after its founder is gone, a company's original values will live on, having withstood the test of time.

I agree with this line of thinking. But companies are not unlike people: while values may be established early on, life experience is their true test. Certain values may not become apparent until a situation brings them to the forefront. Throughout its life span, a company's values should be revisited and reexamined.

Even if the values and purpose of an organization don't change over time, its strategies, structure, products, and markets should. As Jim Collins notes, "Enduring great companies preserve their core values and purpose while their business strategies and operating practices endlessly adapt to a changing world."[4] At FWI, we know that the integrity of our information is at our core. We have changed or expanded how we produce and disseminate our content, who we produce content for and why, and strategies for how we profitably grow our business in a fiercely competitive marketplace. But without the quality and integrity of our content, we would cease to exist as FWI.

To summarize, in Accountable Organizations values and purpose are driven by leadership—not by committee. Values and purpose statements must be unique, meaningful, and inspiring to the organization. Finally, the leadership must continually find ways to instill, communicate, and reinforce its guiding principles throughout the culture, both in words and actions. If reinforced and embraced by senior management, an organization's values and purpose can serve as powerful litmus tests for all stakeholders when planning and executing, when challenged with conflict, or when confronted with fork-in-the-road decisions.

Seeing into the Future: An Exercise

About once a year, I use this simple process to engage myself in the mind-set of a dreamer. It takes less than an hour of uninterrupted time. Get paper, a pencil, and a calculator (or a laptop) and find a comfortable spot to think about and answer the questions below.

1. Pick a date five to ten years in the future.

2. Look at your current annual revenue, and multiply that amount by ten.

3. Now, let that date and revenue number transport you to the future. Having reached this level of success, what does your business look like? Get descriptive. How many employees do you have? How big are your facilities? What does your product mix look like? Who are your customers? As with any brainstorming exercise, don't edit your thoughts. Just write them down.

4. After you've finished, ask yourself the most important question: "What did I have to do to get here?"

5. From the future's perspective, look back at all that has happened over the years to bring your company to its present success. What kinds of milestones will you have passed? What kinds of major decisions will you have made? Looking back, what will have been your "big break"? You may choose to plot these milestones along a timeline that spans from today to the future date you've chosen.

You'll know that the exercise has been particularly powerful when you see that your company's values and purpose have been maintained—even strengthened—along the entire timeline. With some alterations, this exercise can be used to gain clarity in any context, no matter where you are in an organization. For example, say you are a product director for a $50 million brand. Give yourself a time frame of seven years and multiply by ten. First, you may find the *entire* market for your product today is only $200 million. How do you get to $500 million? Should you grow the market? Do you need a line extension? How much share can you grab from competitors? Can you market your product globally? Whatever your situation, find a way to set the future, create the multiple, describe that future reality, and then look at the steps that got you there. In this particular example, when you're typically focused tactically on annual plans and making your quarterly numbers, you will be surprised at how "thinking big" changes your perspective.

If you find yourself stuck when it comes to envisioning your future, throw out the money aspect. A friend of mine once had me pull out a piece of paper and sketch out my ideal organizational structure two to three years in the future, with money as no object. Specific names were not important, just general ideas of groups, departments, leaders. At the end of the exercise, I had in front of me a structure that had far more breadth and depth than I would have constructed hire-by-hire going forward. With this aspirational structure in front of me, I could then *go back* and see who the next hires would be within a larger strategy.

Exercises like these can help spark your creativity. Even if you don't consider yourself a visionary, you have the ability to paint an inspiring picture of your organization's future success. Consider using this kind of exercise every year as you go through your planning process.

Testing Clarity: When It Means
Walking Away from Money

Defining your values and purpose, while challenging, is the easy part. One of the true challenges is when money is on the line. I encountered this test early on in FWI's history. As related earlier, fearing for my company's very existence, I took on a project when I had no business doing so. The episode resulted in no financial gain and a damaged relationship to boot. It was a good lesson, though, and one of the key reasons FWI has continued to thrive.

A significant portion of our business consists of providing physicians with the latest research and product news affecting their specialty. Physicians don't pay to receive these updates; rather, they are funded through contracts we have with health care companies. Though they're writing the checks, the companies we contract with relinquish editorial control. They pay us to deliver true educational value to physicians—not to be a mouthpiece for their marketing departments. How do we get for-profit companies to go along with this?

Like everyone else, physicians are skeptical. They have become trained to look for the angle, the pitch. However, what they receive from us are objective, unbiased updates about what's going on in their specialty. Even though the sponsoring company is clearly identified, it's just as clear that what's being communicated is news the physician can use. Sometimes what's making the news isn't flattering to the sponsoring company's drug. Sometimes the news involves competing drugs. We report it all as objectively and accurately as possible.

Time-strapped physicians appreciate how these updates help them stay abreast of what's happening in their specialties: groundbreaking research, health policy developments, actions by the Food and Drug Administration. They appreciate the quality of the editorial direction and writing. But above all, they appreciate that a health care company (often pharmaceuticals) would have the insight and intellectual honesty to sponsor such a service. The approach that FWI takes in helping health care companies support physicians is focused on building trust. In our opinion, there is no better way to build a brand.

It can be a tough sell. First and foremost, the job of marketers is to increase sales of their product; it makes sense that they'd instinctively want to control the messaging associated with their product. With our services, that message is subtle: it's one of trust, born of the sponsoring company's desire to help physicians do their job better—even if it means letting them know that a competitor's drug has value, too. Similarly, FWI's partnerships with its sponsoring companies are founded on trust. These relationships take time to cultivate—sometimes years. We have to earn our partners' business by proving our trustworthiness and commitment to quality.

If we abandoned that differentiating factor, we'd be throwing our hat into the ring with thousands of other companies that promise their clients flat-out messaging—pure advertising without the goal of developing trust-based relationships. As a former pharmaceutical marketer myself, I know there is a place for this kind of promotion. However, by clinging to our objectivity, FWI offers companies the opportunity to provide physicians with something truly special: differentiated value based on objective information and trust.

Bottom line: If we didn't walk away from contracts that would compromise our objectivity, we'd lose our edge. We'd lose what differentiated us as a valued partner both to the health care industry and to physicians. We'd throw away what got us to being able to say no in the first place.

Integrity is a challenge not only to attain, but also to maintain. It means sticking to your guns and turning down business that would compromise your organization's values and purpose. Companies that don't know how to say no will find it difficult to earn trust—after all, how can customers trust a company when they don't know what it stands for?

From Plan to Action

Accountable Organizations are clear about who they are and what they aspire to achieve. Gaining clarity means setting the parameters for accountable decision making: choices are made based on what your company believes in, not what sounds good at the time. Similarly, once defined, values and purpose set the stage for creating a meaningful strategic plan, which is discussed in chapter 5.

BUILDING THE ACCOUNTABLE ORGANIZATION

1. Evaluate your company's current values, mission, and vision (or purpose) statements.

   - How well do these statements characterize the meaning behind your organization's existence? Do they inspire you?

   - Are they specific to your company, or could they describe any company?

   - What is the level of awareness and understanding within your organization regarding these statements? How are your values and purpose reinforced throughout the company?

2. Do your answers indicate a need to better communicate your company's values and purpose? Or, do you see a need to reevaluate your organizational values and purpose? If so, what strategies can you identify for prompting change?

3. Consider your own personal values and purpose. Are they consistent with those of your organization? If not, how do you reconcile the difference—or can you?

CHAPTER FIVE

EXECUTION
Implementing Strategy with Commitment and Discipline

Identifying your values and purpose is the essential first step in building an Accountable Organization. Once defined, they shouldn't languish on a plaque—they must be integrated into the next critical step: strategic planning. You need a plan that works and the ability to work the plan.

A Road Map for Clarity and Accountability

A rigorous planning process that is in tune with your values and purpose allows all stakeholders to remain focused on their core business. Accountable Organizations require a consistent process and methodology for execution; without it, companies jump from initiative to initiative, appearing unfocused to both customers and employees. Aside from the obvious short-term costs associated with missed opportunities, failed projects, and inefficient implementation, companies without focus will struggle with accountability and trust. Management consultant Robert Shaw observes,

> *If an organization's strategic focus and business priorities constantly change, it will never earn the trust of those who work either within the organization or with it. Leaders should take note: They too must keep their strategic focus and business priorities steady in order to be trusted. When organizations and their leaders seek results at any cost, the trust they need for long term financial performance will be eroded.*[1]

The sequential logic in effective planning is the same at most companies: assessing the current state of business (situation analysis), determining your obstacles and opportunities, then breaking down the steps to achieving the plan (strategies, tactics, actions). A strong strategic plan serves as the ultimate frame of reference, the common measuring stick for everyone in your organization. It allows the company's activities to be compared against its values, thus upholding integrity.

One innovative approach to strategic planning is described by Gordon Shaw, Robert Brown, and Philip Bromily in an influential article for the *Harvard Business Review*. The authors report how storytelling has been integrated into planning at various parts of 3M, resulting in what is called "strategic narratives"—"not only to clarify the thinking behind their plans but also to capture the imagination and the excitement of the people in their organizations."[2]

As the article points out, strategic narratives allow for easier detection of leaps of faith and logic, allowing for quicker remedies. Each plan is unmistakably specific to its company. And most important, the story that the narrative strategy tells—complete with setting, dramatic conflict, and resolution—truly inspires the reader. Where bullets leave empty gaps, a strategic narrative fleshes out relationships. Its authors and readers have a personal stake in its story, for they are among its cast of characters. Shaw and his coauthors conclude,

> *A well-written narrative strategy that shows a difficult situation and an innovative solution leading to improved market share can be galvanizing—and it is certainly more engaging than a bulleted mandate to "increase market share by 5%." When people can locate themselves in the story, their sense of commitment and involvement is enhanced. By conveying a powerful impression of the process of winning, narrative plans can motivate and mobilize an entire organization.*[3]

One further point on strategic narratives: It's said that short stories are the most difficult to write—the format requires precision and economy of language. However, a well-crafted short story can be more compelling than a rambling full-length novel. I believe the same is true when it comes to writing a strategic narrative: precision and economy are important. If you can't limit your narrative to ten or fifteen pages, you've probably littered it with clutter and cloudy thinking. Once you have the narrative completed, you can summarize its vital components for quick reference and tracking progress.

Whatever your approach, your strategic plan needs buy-in from all members of the organization to be meaningful. This is a common challenge for companies, particularly large ones. While your organization may be masterful at planning, it may not be as effective at execution. At FWI, we've incorporated our annual goals and objectives and our values and purpose statements on a single page. Every employee has a copy of our strategic plan and receives a monthly update on our progress. Communication is vital in turning the strategic plan into reality, but it's not enough. To successfully implement your plan, you must also gain the commitment of everyone it relies on.

Internal Commitment

After you have determined your objective and strategies, it's important to get your constituents involved in putting together the execution elements of your plan. Encourage your employees to be involved in a collaborative process of setting measurable tactics and actions. Recalling an executive's insight from chapter 2, it's a mistake to hand down these portions of the plan from atop the mountain: "You can invite [accountability], but I don't think you can impose it on somebody . . . and if you believe you can, then I think you're setting up a situation for failure." Moreover, these people have the first-hand knowledge and in-the-trenches insight that get the job done.

Managers have always asked themselves, "How do I get my people committed to producing results?" We can say we're accountable for what we do, but do we really believe it? As Harvard professor Chris Argyris argues, to be fully accountable, employees need to be *internally committed* to achieving the results. As his wording implies, this means the drive is coming from within the individual: "Internal commitment is created when individuals have significant influence on defining the goals to be achieved and the paths required to achieve them, when the goals represent a significant (but not insurmountable) challenge, and when all these are related to the central values and the needs of the individual."[4] In other words, people need to be a part of the process, and what they're working on must be meaningful to them. More often than not, however, managers get *external commitment* from employees. The difference, says Argyris, is that

> *when someone else defines objectives, goals, and the steps to be taken to reach them, whatever commitment exists will be external. . . . Internal commitment is different. It requires not the acquiescence, but the participation of employees in defining both goals and performance standards.*[5]

If what you want is internally committed employees who are fully accountable for their actions—in other words, if you want breakthrough results—don't pay lip service to buy-in. In fact, when companies thrust accountability onto employees, results are marginal at best. This final point from Argyris is worth repeating at length (emphasis mine):

> *Difficulties commonly arise when managers espouse values and actions consistent with [internal commitment] but implement programs, that are, in fact, consistent with [external commitment]. The inner contradiction comes alive largely when implementation efforts begin. Managed poorly, such contradictions can rip an organization apart. Ironically, what often prevents a blowup is that employees learn to live with the inconsistencies by* quietly distancing themselves from feeling responsible for continually energizing the programs. *This may prevent disaster, but it sacrifices the upside potential of a fully engaged cohort of employees.*
>
> *No wonder so many reenergizing initiatives have proven disappointing. Notwithstanding the rhetoric of internal commitment, the lower one looks in an organization undergoing reengineering, the more conditions are consistent with external commitment. This is, no doubt, an important part of the reason why such processes have had, at best, limited positive consequences and, more often, have decreased management's credibility.*[6]

If employees are "quietly distancing themselves from feeling responsible," you've got an accountability problem. No matter what the management rhetoric, people will lose interest in the tasks at hand if they didn't play a role in defining them. As initiatives sputter and die time and again, employees will assuredly lose trust in the leadership of an organization.

Argyris's point about commitment provides a word of warning to those who read this book, find the concepts useful, and go back to their organization ready to "implement" the processes described. Even if you are in a leadership position, you can't walk in the door and cram accountability down people's throats. In implementing any organizational change—as with the goal-setting process—you need to build credibility and buy-in at a grass-roots level. It takes time.

What's crucial—and worth repeating, since it's so often forgotten—is the collaborative nature of the execution part of planning. Only with collaboration will you earn full, internal commitment and accountability from your employees, a primary tenet of the Accountable Organization.

Practice Like You Play

I have a good friend who has played on the professional women's tennis tour. I've always wondered, what's the difference that makes the difference? What separates the number one tennis player in the world from number ten, from number one hundred, and then, from a club pro? The first time I played tennis with my friend, I noticed that during her warm-up she was running down every ball. I mean, *every* ball, no matter where I hit it. After watching her chase my stray shots for ten minutes, I had to ask the question: Why? "I *hate* to let the ball get past me," she replied. At some point, probably as a child, she had learned that every ball counts—whether it's game day or not.

One of the managers on my executive team coaches little league baseball. He'll often bring up gems from how he coaches his kids, and invariably there is some application to business management. "Practice like you play," he once said, having recently watched a few of our salespeople—who are naturally great on their feet—turn in a shoddy performance at an important internal meeting. Rambling through their presentations, unprepared, it was if they were telling the rest of us, "So what? We only turn up the juice when it matters."

I don't mean to pick on my salespeople, but it *does* matter. In my former job, I wouldn't dare get up in front of my colleagues without being totally prepared. As far as I was concerned, it was game day every day; things haven't changed in my role at FWI. At that meeting, part of what I was seeing was a lack of internal commitment. The sales team hadn't bought into the process; they didn't understand the importance and so they winged it.

Moreover, they had forgotten that, as the saying goes, how you do anything is how you do everything. In other words, they forgot that last, crucial element of effective execution: discipline. After strategy and internal commitment, finally there is the personal work ethic. Like integrity, it's something we can spot in other people, and something we admire. If you've got it, you have a leg up in this world. If you don't, you might ask yourself why—and take a hard look at how it's holding you back from realizing your potential.

Leadership: Navigating the Accountable Organization

As we have seen, leaders set the vision and purpose for Accountable Organizations. They direct the strategic planning and encourage internal commitment among employees. CEOs in particular are the ones who are ultimately accountable for an organization's success or failure. But they also have a crucial role in building trust. Chapter 6 discusses how the many roles that CEOs play affect trust, and provide some practical advice for emerging leaders of—and within—Accountable Organizations.

BUILDING THE
ACCOUNTABLE ORGANIZATION

1. Consider the strategic narrative approach to planning and create a one-page "story" about your company. Illustrate your history, the people, your products, your competitive space, and your business strategy. Describe your critical success factors for the next twelve months. Based on your narrative, have you discovered any "red flags" that need immediate attention? Share your narrative with colleagues and elicit feedback.

2. Many companies undergo a rigorous planning process but find it difficult to execute those plans. At your own firm, what are the biggest barriers to implementation? Are there certain initiatives that falter year after year, and if so, why?

3. Do the members of your work group or team seek internal commitment on projects? If so, what are the processes you use to gain buy-in? What other ways can you think of to increase internal commitment among subordinates, colleagues, and superiors?

CHAPTER SIX

LEADERSHIP
Navigating Context,
Fulfilling Many Roles

Lee Iacocca was the first CEO in recent times to be internationally recognized for his leadership, grace, and guts. He was able to pull Chrysler from the brink of death, taking his charisma to Washington and successfully selling Congress on a government-backed bailout. He improved quality at a time when American cars were the butt of many jokes. In the end, Iacocca was synonymous with the Chrysler brand. His fight for the company's survival brought him unprecedented media attention, and his style won over many Americans. His book *Iacocca: An Autobiography* became a best-seller. A new kind of American icon—the celebrity CEO—was born.

The Celebrity CEO

In his book *Searching for a Corporate Savior*, Harvard Business School professor Rakesh Khurana talks about the emergence of the charismatic CEO:

> *The new corporate leadership that began emerging in the 1980s was in many ways a throwback to the swashbuck-ling Robber Barons of the late nineteenth century. This group, however, tended to be more public-relations savvy and psychologically attuned to the zeitgeist, thus avoid-ing being vilified as the Robber Barons had been. . . . These new members of the business elite were no longer defined as professional managers but instead as leaders, whose ability to lead consisted in their personal charac-teristics or, more simply, their charisma.*[1]

The stock market boom of the late 1990s—and particu-larly the dot-com phenomenon—further perpetuated the celebrity CEO culture. The new high-profile leaders tended to be from technology-related companies: Bill Gates of Microsoft, Steve Jobs of Apple and Pixar, Lou Gerstner of IBM, Michael Dell of Dell Computer, Carly Fiorina of Hewlett-Packard, Jeff Bezos of Amazon, and Larry Ellison of Oracle, among others. With the democratization of the stock market and skyrocket-ing share prices, the public fawned over these charismatic new masters of the universe.

According to economist Robert Shiller, management in the 1990s was about boosting share price above all else, due in large part to the emerging power of the institutional investor. CEOs were given strong incentives to keep that focus, including stock options. Shiller comments,

> *This new selection and incentive method for top management is a grand social experiment that turned managers into market manipulators, shifting their focus towards acting out phony new-paradigm fantasies, boosting the market price at the expense of real fundamental value, and even occasionally fudging earnings.[2]*

One could say, then, that CEOs of public companies in those years were paid handsomely to spin the market for the benefit of shareholders. But to be fair, perhaps we were happy to be spun as long as we were watching our retirement funds grow. Perhaps we weren't being completely honest, then, when we claimed to be shocked by the scandals in corporate America—CEOs talking up company stock to employees while discreetly dumping it themselves, disgraced executives taking the Fifth, massaged numbers, massive bankruptcies. Rather than ask probing questions and possibly discover that the emperor had no clothes, we wanted to believe in the "new-paradigm fantasies."

Of course, there are charismatic CEOs who have been truly successful in leading their organizations. The turnaround stories of Gerstner at IBM and Jobs at Apple are indeed inspiring tales of effective leadership. But countless other charismatic CEOs have proven to be ineffective—and at their worst, self-interested and unethical. As stakeholders in Accountable

Organizations, we must demand more from our leadership than a winning smile and an ability to manage a press conference.

What Does It Mean to Be a Leader?

Recently, a simple Google search on "leadership" yielded 11.7 million Web destinations; refining the search to "leadership in business" narrowed the number down to a mere 3.9 million. Moving on to Amazon.com, I found 12,694 books on leadership for sale and about half as many books on leadership in business.

The numbers speak for themselves—we are obsessed with finding out what it means to be an effective leader. Leadership is the single most written-about topic in business. It dominates books about history and politics. Every day, leaders are analyzed, prodded, lambasted, and occasionally praised by the media. Over the years, I've seen effective leadership described as an art as well as a science, as Machiavellian, as being a servant of the people, as charismatic, as pragmatic, as primal, as quiet. The bookshelves overflow with leadership fables, leadership primers, leadership laws, even one-minute leadership guides.

I'll admit, the prospect of writing this chapter was daunting. So much has been written on leadership—what could I possibly add that hasn't already been written? Consider what some of the best business thinkers have contributed on the topic:

Warren Bennis: *"[Leaders] know who they are, what their strengths and weaknesses are, and how to fully deploy their strengths and compensate for their weaknesses. They* *also know what they want, why they want it, and how to communicate what they want to others, in order to achieve their goals."*[3]

Daniel Goleman: *"Great leaders move us. They ignite our passion and inspire the best in us. When we try to explain why they are so effective, we speak of strategy, vision, or powerful ideas. But the reality is much more primal: Great leadership works through the emotions."*[4]

Peter Senge: *"[What distinguishes leaders] is the clarity and persuasiveness of their ideas, the depth of their commitment, and their openness to continually learning more. They do not 'have the answer.' But they do instill confidence in those around them that together, 'we can learn whatever we need to learn in order to achieve the results we truly desire.'"*[5]

By definition, a leader is someone who has followers. We all know it's this simple, and that's part of the reason why leadership is so fascinating. Leadership strikes at our desire for power—but not necessarily power as it relates to competition. Power can also be about influence, about making a difference. We are social creatures, and we want to leave our mark. We all want the power to impact others, and the best way is to influence the societies we move within—to get the attention of those around us and move them to action.

After reading scores of books, after heading up my own company, after mentoring and coaching other CEOs, and after attending more than my share of seminars, I do know this:

There isn't one "right way" of leading an Accountable Organization. It depends on who you are as a person. It depends on the people you're leading—who they are and how many there are of them. In other words, your effectiveness as a leader—both in inspiring action and building trust—largely depends on how you navigate *context.*

An Early Lesson in Leadership

At an early age, I was intrigued by what made a person successful—what defined a "winner." However, I didn't truly understand what it meant to be a leader, not until I reached college. Having played competitive tennis for years, I arrived at Knox College my freshman year cocky and ready to rule the team. I thought no one could beat me, and the first few weeks of preseason practice proved me right. In my mind, there was no doubt: based on my skills, I was the best player on the team.

Yet when it came time to elect the team captain, I wasn't the one they chose. Instead, the team elected my friend Chris. And when the season opened, I found myself in the number two singles spot—not number one. I was confused, wondering if somehow I didn't understand how college tennis worked. My coach sat me down for a talk. "John," he said, "being captain of the team is a leadership position, as is being our number one singles player. In order to be captain of this team, you need to be a leader off the court as well as on it. Right now, I see that you're neither."

I was furious. What was he talking about? I thought, if you're the best, you play number one. Besides, how was I not leading on court? Leading meant winning, which I had proven I knew how to do. As far as my off-court behavior was concerned, that was none of his business.

Of course, the story of my off-court behavior that first year in college was typical. Fall term was such a disaster that I nearly flunked out. By the time tennis season rolled around that spring and "freshmanitis" had run its course, I had straightened up my act off-court, but my on-court behavior left much to be desired. I swore, threw my racquet, and on the sidelines didn't do much to support my team members. I showed no reverence for the seniors on the team, believing I could drill them in my sleep. Looking back, I'm ashamed of my arrogance.

Fortunately, not long into the season I finally got the message. I was digging myself out of a hole in a long, three-set match. I'd come from behind after losing the first set, and was trailing in the third. The points were long. My opponent refused to miss; I was earning my points only by hitting outright winners after long, tiring rallies. I was the last of my team on court—everyone else had finished their matches long ago.

I was so in the zone of the match that it took a while before I noticed: none of my teammates were there on the sidelines. Some were eating sandwiches in the van, others were cracking jokes by the concession stand. At 4-4 in the third set, there wasn't a single player from my team behind the fence supporting me. On the other hand, it appeared that virtually every player from my opponent's team was there watching, as was their coach. No wonder I hadn't heard any cheers when I won a point.

Finally, I won the match. Exhausted, I sat down on the court with a towel over my head, dousing myself with cold water. Maybe it was the emotional roller coaster of a long match. More likely, it was the realization that my teammates couldn't stand me. I cried into my towel.

That day, after I finished feeling sorry for myself, I made the decision to change. The only way I would earn the right to be a team leader was to start acting like one—by showing respect and earning my teammates' trust. It didn't happen overnight, but I learned to do what my instincts told me was right. I did my best to support my teammates in practice and in competition. I cleaned up my language and avoided rude behavior on court. I considered myself a representative of both my team and school, whether we were competing at home or away.

About midseason, my coach played me at the number one spot—and for nearly every match from that point on, that's where I remained for the rest of my college career. I finally understood that leadership is not just defined by competition, but also—and often more important—by respecting others and earning their trust. Pure skill isn't enough . . . If you want to lead, you must provide people with a compelling reason to follow.

The CEO and the Accountable Organization

That lesson in leadership has stayed with me ever since, through graduate school, jobs in corporate America, starting and growing my own company. Through these experiences, I've discovered that effective leaders understand the many different roles they play within their organization. Even though their styles may differ, effective leaders understand how these roles uniquely affect their ability to inspire action and build trust.

So, as you read the following sections, think about how you approach these different roles. Which come naturally, and which do you struggle with? Which would you rather forget? While I discuss these roles from a CEO's perspective—and include specific recommendations for the chief executive—how you tackle the underlying issues will shape your effectiveness as a leader no matter where you are in the company's hierarchy.

The Humanitarian

CEOs make decisions with the collective interest of their organization at heart. That means people matter—they deserve an environment in which they are treated with dignity and respect. The people in an organization aren't just tools to get work done; they're not pieces on a chessboard to be played off one another. A company is the collective endeavor of people—without them, the computers and machinery stand idle and the business plans gather dust. The same is true for manufacturing firms, telecommunications providers, and any other business one can think of. As trite as it may sound, while the direction and strategy may come from above, it's the employees' passion and commitment that produce a superior product or service.

Because of this, the position of chief executive officer carries with it an enormous humanitarian responsibility. Profits cannot be put ahead of people. I believe that CEOs have a moral imperative to remember that their decisions affect the lives of everyone in the organization, and their families as well. As someone described it to me, "Great leaders view themselves as stewards. Great leaders see themselves as being in service to the people they lead." At a very fundamental level, this genuine sense of humility, compassion, responsibility, and respect for others inspires people's trust. As I look back to my freshman year in college, I had lacked all these virtues as an aspiring team leader.

But this responsibility also often places leaders in a difficult position, where the choice is between the lesser of two evils. Harvard Business School professor Joseph Badaracco calls these decisions "defining moments."[6] Consider this example: One of your product lines is so unprofitable that it's driving the company into the ground. You have made the decision to eliminate the product line, and with it, you'll be laying off four hundred people at the first of the year. It's now just after Thanksgiving, and you haven't yet made the announcement, because your board has advised you to wait until after the holidays—a premature announcement would affect vendor orders for your other product lines in the coming year. You are approached at the holiday party by one of the people on the production line who had heard a rumor about the product being killed and is concerned about what to spend for this year's Christmas gifts. What do you do?

This situation represents a common dilemma that managers and leaders face. It also manifests itself in situations among colleagues. As Badaracco says, it's a choice between "right" and "right." Should you tell the employee the truth, so that he can responsibly budget for the holidays? Absolutely. Do you have a responsibility to the organization and its stakeholders to remain quiet, as a premature release of the news would negatively affect sales companywide? Definitely. Because people are involved, your role as humanitarian requires that you don't make these choices lightly. They are, indeed, your defining moments as a leader. Ultimately, right vs. right decisions are a test of the leader's integrity: they require a careful deliberation of the facts, considering of underlying moral principles and values, acting in accordance with those principles, and communicating the decision in a meaningful way.

The Sage

A leader must also be a sage: a coach, a teacher-learner, a mentor. All of these elements are related, yet they require different approaches to helping others achieve understanding and reach their goals. As the coach—an overused sports metaphor that nonetheless continues to stand the test of time—you're the head of the team, making decisions, charting strategy, getting the most out of every player. As a teacher-learner, you have a wealth of experience and knowledge to share with others; you also seek to learn from everyone else, as they have different skills, experience, and expertise than you do. Finally, as a mentor, you nurture others at their own pace, helping them be the best they can be. In all these roles, you earn trust by willingly giving of yourself to help others advance.

Early on in my career I was lucky enough to have a great mentor who immediately asked me, "What's going to be your first victory? How I can help you get there?" I learned so much from this person, and indeed achieved my first "victory" with his help. This idea has stuck with me to this day: Make sure that you mentor new employees in a manner that allows them to complete a project of notoriety, an accomplishment that boosts their confidence right away. It sets people off on the right foot. Then, help people build on their victories. In addition to helping others move ahead, you are fulfilling a responsibility to the wider organization to create its future leaders. Without coaching, teaching, and mentoring, you leave the cultivation of the organization's internal leadership to chance.

Of course, there is another aspect to being a sage, embodied in the image of the wise old person on top of the mountain, the one to whom others come for counsel. You won't immediately have all the answers—and that's all right. Trust is earned by your willingness to carefully consider and deliberate on a problem until you come to an answer. It's earned by understanding that, as CEO, your opinion carries disproportionate weight in the organization—indeed, it may be the final word in a dispute. So, earn trust through impartiality and honest deliberation.

The Deal Maker

Former CEO and executive coach Walt Sutton puts it this way: One of the functions of the CEO is "to navigate the rivers of cash."[7] That means evaluating all the deals in front of you and deciding which ones to greenlight and which ones to take a pass on. Remember Iacocca marching off to Washington to put together the deal of the century, the one that would literally save his company? It's possible you may find yourself staring down a deal that will be the making of your company. Most of the time, however, the deals you evaluate will represent a wide range of opportunities: strategic alliances, partnerships, new products.

I absolutely support a culture of innovation at FWI. But truth be told, most of our product ideas come from the customers themselves. And that's not a bad thing—it's a great thing. By my definition, marketing means figuring out what the customer needs and wants, and then satisfying that need or desire better than anyone else. Conducting product development in a vacuum is a big mistake. Having customers influence your product development efforts is crucial to staying in tune with market needs.

And this is why you need to stay in front of customers—
that you continue to earn their trust—even if you're the CEO,
and even if you're not serving customers day to day. It's been
said that when Lou Gerstner started at IBM, the first thing he
did was get on an airplane. Where was he going? To see the
CEO of each major account. He was on a mission to learn
what his customers wanted from IBM, which at the time was
apparently not what they were getting. The visits also carried
an underlying message: The buck stopped with Lou.

While I don't directly manage accounts anymore, I still
visit customers, listening to their ideas and offering myself as
a resource to solve problems and identify opportunities. I let
our clients know that I'm there, and ultimately they can trust
that the buck stops with me.

The Risk Taker

Chapter 9 is dedicated to the topic of risk, so here I will be brief.
Nonetheless, it's important to emphasize that, as CEO, your
role as chief risk taker is crucial to your company's survival.

However, it can be a difficult role to embrace. Sales are up,
profits are up, and your bonus is up—so why rock the boat?
Or you may be facing the opposite situation, telling yourself,
"I can't afford to take risks with net income down 10 percent!"
Maybe you're somewhere in the middle—your profits climb a
predictable 3 percent a year no matter what you do. Or maybe
it has little to do with how your company is doing—you're at
the pinnacle of your career and are content with collecting a

paycheck and playing golf four times a week. That's understandable . . . you worked for it, right? Now, why don't you just quit right now and do your company a favor?

CEOs are paid to take risks. Educated and responsible risks, yes, but risks nonetheless. As you set the vision and make the deals, be conscientious, keeping in mind that your people are counting on you. But don't let the weight of responsibility cow you into risk avoidance.

Similarly, part of the CEO's role as risk taker is played out *within* the organization—by making changes in order to keep your people fresh, motivated, and productive. How you approach this role greatly influences buy-in and trust. Consider the response inspired by the typical announcement that a company is "embarking on a new era," and that employees should "be prepared for some big changes on the horizon." Look out at the audience and what do you see? The ones who are still there are frozen in their chairs, staring back with terror in their eyes. Why? People fear change; they fear the unknown.

When seeking to create buy-in as you effect change, why not reframe the process as "experimentation"? Next time you want to do something differently, tell your team that you are about to experiment with a new idea. Watch the look of anticipation on their faces. You'll have an audience of curious learners, ready to roll up their sleeves and try something new. It's necessary to "shock the system" every once in a while, to get people to think differently. If you get them on board up front, it will be much easier to take the risk—and make your next breakthrough.

When was the last time you shocked your system?

The Manager

When I think of *manager* in the traditional sense, I think *technician*—they're the ones who are experts in planning, analysis, measurement of outcomes, and control. Meanwhile, the word *leader* has come to embody an elusive inspirational quality—leaders are the ones who move people. Nonetheless, leaders can learn a great deal from effective managers. As head of an organization, it's vital to understand how to manage people as well as motivate them, because managerial competence is a powerful way to earn trust.

In my own case, when it comes to management I'm as good a generalist as any, having a solid understanding of marketing, finance, and operations. It's also true that everyone at FWI is better at their job than I would be; you wouldn't want me putting together the company's tax return. But I know enough about the functional areas of the business not to be scared to read a financial report, and I know enough to manage by exception. Most of the time I know what to look for, and since the buck indeed does stop with me, I'd better pay attention to the details.

This isn't only true for small companies. At IBM, Lou Gerstner was good on his feet, he was a visionary, and he cared about the people in his company. But he also was a highly competent technician. Bill Gates still reviews lines of code. It's not enough to have charisma. Great CEOs act like managers—they roll up their sleeves and get their hands dirty. They get involved.

Being involved takes keen observation. If you're the CEO, you can't rely solely on information that comes to you through the traditional channels: meetings, e-mail, reports, even casual conversations. Why? Because people hate to deliver disappointing results to supervisors, no matter how graciously those supervisors take the news. On the other hand, people may overstate their victories. Of course, these concerns lessen as trust within an organization increases, but it is just human nature to want to present the best picture to one's boss.

Finally, part of the role of manager entails orchestrating a steady improvement in performance. The quality of most rank-and-file employees, managers, and executives will cycle in an up-and-down fashion. It's rare that the stellar performer can maintain that high level of excellence day in and day out. Nonetheless, when looking at performance growth conceptually—whether it's a person's technical competence or emotional competence—what you're looking for is something akin to the Dow Jones Industrial Average over a long period of time. Sure, there will be some bumps in the road, maybe even a recession from time to time, but the graph continues to trend upward. Your job as a manager is to minimize the peaks and valleys. You're looking for steady, predictable growth.

The reason for managing the troughs is intuitive, but why manage the peaks? To avoid burnout. Your star performers are most susceptible to this, being so achievement oriented that they work around the clock—until they get burned out and crash, that is. As much as you monitor for dips in your team's performance, pay equally close attention to the stars. When a star is burned out, it doesn't give off any heat. Keep your stars healthy and shining.

The Motivator

"I think leaders need to appreciate the context of the broader relationship system," says David Wolfenden, a leadership coach and executive at DMB, a real estate development company.

> *As a leader, you have less latitude to publicly walk up and start talking to somebody in an irritated voice than someone else might—not because it's inherently wrong, but because the context of leadership requires you to be more compassionate and sensitive to the broader relationship system in which the conversation occurs, which includes the past, present, and future.*[8]

In other words, as a leader you can't afford to let your distemper get the best of you, because the people who surround you will take on your disposition like mood rings. You cannot escape from this reality, but you can use it to your organization's advantage. CEOs can motivate employees in ways that no one else can. At FWI, if I'm positive and upbeat, so are those around me. While that may be a known psychological phenomenon about humans in general—enthusiasm is contagious—it's especially true when it comes from the CEO.

What about integrity, you say? If you're in a bad mood and you put on a false front, isn't that less than honest? Well, yes; if you walk around with a silly grin all day, every day, people will wonder if it's time to have you taken away. Or, at the least, they'll become distrustful of your demeanor. I'm not talking about constantly masking your emotions. People like to know that their CEO is human as well. But one of the hallmarks of "emotionally intelligent" leaders is their ability to understand how their emotions affect others and to manage those emotions appropriately.[9] It's fine if you have a bad day. Just don't make it a habit, and be acutely aware of the effect that your moods have on others. Your enthusiasm pays dividends down the line.

Ask yourself: Why did you take the job of CEO in the first place? Maybe you're like me—you founded the place. Maybe you were hired or promoted to the job. It really doesn't matter how you got there, but as the chief motivator, you've got to have *passion* for what you do and what your company does. If you've lost your passion, figure out a way to get it back, and quickly. Indifference is as contagious as enthusiasm, and the last thing you need is a company full of people who just don't care.

The Visionary

The "vision thing" is so obvious I hesitate to mention it—it's what many CEOs consider to be their *only* role. But for every visionary CEO I've met, there are two who haven't an idea as to where they're headed. And that's unfortunate, because defining the company's vision is the one role that the leader absolutely cannot delegate.

There have been times during my tenure when the future looked uncertain, such as during FWI's rebranding. Yet that process has helped me to establish a clear vision for the company. I went back and revisited our roots; I talked to customers; I talked to people who had looked at our product but hadn't purchased, and asked why; I held internal focus groups; and I hired a branding agency for guidance. I asked for employees' input. But the final call—the decision about what and who we would aspire to be—was up to me.

Again, some CEOs believe in determining their company's vision by committee, because they want buy-in from their employees. It's their company, too, they say, so everyone should have their stamp on it. It's an admirable sentiment. I, too, believe in getting buy-in from employees and asking for their opinions. However, when you get too large a group of people together expressly to create a statement of vision (or values, or purpose, or mission), you end up with something that's less than inspirational. Having been stretched to accommodate everyone's stamp, the statement eventually becomes meaningless.

I don't mean to dissuade you from soliciting input from your employees. By all means—talk with them, listen to their varied perspectives on what the company means to them. I certainly did and always will. But when it comes to finalizing your company's defining statements, the ultimate decision is yours. Make these statements meaningful, powerful, and easy to remember. Then consistently communicate them to all your company's employees, whether they number fifty or fifty thousand. Of course, this isn't an easy task, even within smaller organizations. However, it is possible to clearly define your organization's values and purpose for employees and consistently reinforce them in creative and memorable ways.

In short, effective CEOs know where they're taking their company. They make their vision memorable, and communicate it with passion.

The Communicator

Ronald Reagan was known as "The Great Communicator." Martin Luther King Jr.'s oratory is legendary. These leaders could electrify their audiences, not only with their words but also their commanding delivery. Leaders who are great public speakers are often referred to as "the voice" of their organization or cause. All great leaders, in fact, seem to have a compelling story to tell. Says Harvard education professor Howard Gardner,

> *Leaders achieve effects primarily by telling stories and by embodying those stories in their own lives. . . . The art of the leader is to create and refine a story so that it engages the attention and commitment of followers, thereby changing their views of who they are, what they committed to, and what they want to achieve and why.*[10]

But the role of the company's CEO as communicator is not limited to making great speeches or keeping the company's story alive. It also encompasses facilitating effective and empathetic communication among all stakeholders in the company. (Chapter 7 includes a detailed discussion on the guideposts for achieving this kind of communication.) "Leaders are responsible for doing as much as they can to create a context where open, rigorous, fair, and balanced discussions are typical," says Craig Weber, an organizational behavior consultant and president of Weber and Associates. "Of course, as the CEO you can't just write a memo and force people to be open, candid, and direct. But you can strive to create a context that promotes openness."[11]

Communicating effectively and empathetically is vital to fostering understanding and buy-in among stakeholders. By creating an environment in which good communication thrives, a leader makes great strides toward building trust.

Committing to Lead, No Matter What Your Title

Effective leaders make a difference. They have the power to influence, and they use that power to build trust. If you're at the top of the organizational chart, that power is built into your position. It's your job to move people to action and create a trusting environment. But as any effective leader knows, a "license to lead" isn't enough. It may give you the authority to direct people in your organization, but it doesn't magically confer the power to inspire them. Only you can develop that power, by being conscious of how you fulfill the different leadership roles outlined above.

Perhaps you're at a place a little lower on the company ladder. Just because you haven't been given a license to lead doesn't mean you don't have that power. You may not be able to dictate strategy, but you can lead in smaller, yet nonetheless important, ways. In fact, members of Accountable Organizations consistently seek opportunities to lead within their spheres of influence. It doesn't take a title to make you a leader. Consider this insight from Joseph Badaracco:

> *The vast majority of difficult, important human problems—both inside and outside organizations—are not solved by a swift, decisive stroke from someone at the top. What usually matters are careful, thoughtful, small, practical efforts by people working far from the limelight. In short, quiet leadership is what moves the world.*[12]

As you go about your business, day in and day out, how do you embrace the different qualities of effective leadership? How do you wield your influence? How do you seek to make a difference? No matter where you are in your organization, you can build trust through your actions. You can show others what it means to be accountable. You can be a guardian of your organization's integrity—and of your own. Whether people follow your lead is not up to them. It's up to you.

BUILDING THE
ACCOUNTABLE ORGANIZATION

1. What was your earliest lesson in what it means to be a leader? What have you always remembered from this lesson, and how does it shape your leadership today?

2. As a leader in your organization, consider the various roles outlined in this chapter. Rating yourself, which of these are your strongest roles, and which are your weakest? What strategies can you employ to improve your performance in these latter roles?

3. Think of the people you admire who exemplify each of the leadership roles. Why do you admire them? What can you learn from them?

CHAPTER SEVEN

COMMUNICATION
Connecting Effectively and with Empathy

In fall 2000, QUALCOMM, Inc., released version 5.0 of its popular Eudora® e-mail program. In addition to other bells and whistles, Eudora 5.0 introduced an optional feature called MoodWatch. As its name suggests, MoodWatch scans both outgoing and incoming e-mail for "potentially offensive language" and issues warnings based on a "three-chili-pepper" scale:

One chili pepper:	"Better hope you know the person."
Two chili peppers:	"Watch out, you're playin' with fire chilies here."
Three chili peppers:	"Whoa, this is the kind of thing that might get your keyboard washed out with soap."

Potential Eudora users are advised: "MoodWatch won't stop you from acting irresponsibly in email, it will just let you know when you might be about to send a message you'll regret."[1]

Being Our Own "Moodwatchers"

MoodWatch is based on rhetorical theories developed by David Kaufer, head of English at Carnegie Mellon University. Kaufer conducted a study of "flaming," which he defines as "computer-mediated communication designed to intimidate the interlocutor by withholding the expected courtesies of polite communication." In other words, flaming is aggressive, angry, or rude language shot across cyberspace at the intended recipient.

According to Kaufer, flaming is all about intimidation. His study, based on an analysis of over one thousand e-mails, produced "dictionaries" of flaming words and phrases that MoodWatch uses in rating individual messages. Of course, there are the usual suspects of profanity and offensive language, but other phrases trigger a "chili alert" simply by their intimidating tone. Examples include "I'm not about to . . ." and "I'm sick and tired of your. . . ."

Of course, as Kaufer notes, a computer program is an imperfect tool. It can detect the "conventional language of flaming," but it can't possibly catch all intimidating language. That's because within the larger context of what's going on in relationships, the most seemingly benign language can come across as outright nasty in an e-mail:

Imagine an employee who is responsible for getting a report out that is late in delivery. The employee's supervisor knows it is late, knows the employee already feels bad it is late and, in a fit of anger, sends the following abrupt email: "When is the report coming out?" The language, on the surface, is an innocent question about the future. Yet the employee feels it as rubbing salt on his wounds, a direct challenge to his fulfillment of his work assignments and, perhaps, his fitness as an employee. The message is meant and deeply felt as a flame, though it bears none of the characteristic linguistic patterns of a flame. No computer program can possibly capture such flaming. Yet the most personally hurtful flames are probably of this type.[2]

Of course, no e-mail monitoring program can fully grasp the complexities of interpersonal relationships. And therein lies one of the greatest limitations of e-mail itself. In this age of multitasking, e-mail is our tool for reaching more people more quickly and frequently than ever before. We don't need to wait for someone to pick up the phone or come out of a meeting. We can be conversing with one person on the phone while at the same time e-mailing another. In other words, if measured by the number of contacts made per unit of time, e-mail has definitely increased the "productivity" of our communication.

But what about the quality? Many have credited e-mail with resurrecting the art of written correspondence. It's true: People to whom letter writing was once a foreign concept are now happily tapping away at their keyboards. But when you factor in e-mail's immediacy, the exchange of messages becomes more telephonic—e-mail becomes another medium for carrying on normal, everyday conversations. However, these conversations are stripped of the usual nonverbal cues to meaning: facial expressions, body language, tone of voice.

So it all comes down to language, to making up for the lack of nonverbal cues with word choice and punctuation. That's tough for us to do when we're conditioned to think of e-mail as the faster way to communicate. Locked in that mindset, we fire off messages left and right, clicking "Send" and assuming the people on the other end are going to understand exactly what we mean. Meanwhile, one of those people clicking "Receive" understands something different entirely. Depending on the miscommunication, the consequences can range from a minor glitch in production to a severely damaged relationship.

Not surprisingly, a new method of mass communication such as e-mail makes us look at how we "talk" to each other using any medium. No matter whether we're e-mailing the boss, catching a colleague in the hallway, or confronting an underperforming employee, as stakeholders we must all be our own "moodwatchers." The responsibility for good communication is ours. With the pressures of time and competition, it is tempting to shortchange this process, to communicate poorly or infrequently. But over time, the consequences of this neglect build up, negatively affecting morale and, ultimately, productivity. In this chapter, we explore the attributes of good communication within Accountable Organizations and without.

Three Guideposts for Communicating Effectively and Empathetically

One of the fundamental rules of management is that if you want to be effective in your job, you must communicate, communicate, communicate. Not only is this true at all levels within an organization—executives, middle management, frontline employees—but it's far better to overcommunicate than to undercommunicate. Unfortunately, most of us do the latter, believing that co-workers are either mind readers or too busy to be bothered. Or we worry that our communications might be unproductive. But the fact is that people don't read minds, nor are they so busy that they don't want or, more important, need to know what's going on. After all, no one can work in a vacuum. So communication cannot be an afterthought; it must be a priority.

Unfortunately, the concept of communication has become an all-encompassing yet meaningless term in business— a catchall without any real teeth. As with integrity, we're all in favor of it. We say we want more of it. We know it when we see it. But can we really define what it means? "Good communication allows any organization—be it a family, team, or business—to identify the challenges that are coming their way and work through them in an efficient way," says Craig Weber. "Everyone has a shared, consistent understanding of what's expected of them."[3]

My father once told me that the single most important factor for success in business was public speaking skills. I think he had a point in that the skill of persuasion gives you leverage; it enables you to move people to action. Thus, part of good communication is effectiveness—closing the deal. And as we all know, that's the game when it comes to business. Getting the other party to sign the dotted line, to meet deadlines, to give his or her best as part of your team. But effectiveness is only half of the equation. After all, yelling can be effective. Lies can be effective, too, as can threats. But these approaches to communication don't do much to cultivate trust in the long term—in fact, they undermine it. So, communication must do more than close the deal; it has to connect. It has to reinforce the ties that make relationships strong and productive; it has to build trust. To accomplish this, communication must be judicious and perceptive. In other words, the second component of good communication is empathy.

Communicating effectively and empathetically is important not only in the context of one-on-one exchange but also in broader applications: departmental and companywide communication, communication with customers, and so on. To maximize trust, all communication must be carried on at eye level, no matter how wide the audience. Whether in written form or verbally, communicate as though you are looking each recipient directly in the eye—whether you're persuading one person or one thousand.

This is, of course, easier said than done. But three guideposts—clarity, consistency, and compassion—will help you to stay on track as you seek to communicate effectively and empathetically within your Accountable Organization.

Clarity

Clear communication is unambiguous. It leaves little or no room for misinterpretation. When you speak and write with clarity, people around you understand that you've identified what is important to you—the first hallmark of integrity. By not being vague, you let your audience know where you stand and that you are accountable for what you're saying. You have nothing to hide.

Be specific. Don't dance around what you mean; get to the heart of it. Again, you cannot assume that the people around you are mind readers. You cannot rely on them to simply "divine" what you want, no matter how big the hints you drop. When you are specific, you do your best to remove uncertainty—the main cause of confusion, fear, and rumor mongering. You show your audience that you trust them enough to be honest with them. If they feel they're getting the straight story, odds are that they'll start feeling comfortable enough to be honest with you, too.

Consistency

Consistency in communication is likely the strongest element when it comes to cultivating trust. Do you communicate to others reliably? Or do you say one thing one day, only to contradict yourself the next? If you send mixed messages, what will your audience assume about you? At the very least, they'll think you haven't thought things through, that you're not sure what you want, that you're flaky. At worst, they'll think you're driven by expediency rather than values, that you're dishonest, that you have no integrity—not the attributes that inspire trust.

When we talk about consistency in communication, frequency inevitably comes up. After all, one's consistency is judged through a succession of communications and actions. If your viewpoint on a certain matter changes over time, your consistency will be called into question if the reasons for this evolution aren't communicated to others—that is, if others are surprised by your change of heart because they had been operating under assumptions that are no longer valid.

Achieving the right frequency of communication is more art than science. If you're like most people, you're not communicating enough. On the other hand—and this is particularly true since the advent of e-mail—remember that we're all suffering from information overload. Use your best judgment and solicit the feedback from co-workers. Do they feel in the know or out in the cold? Work together to achieve the right balance.

Compassion

While logic tells us what is expedient, compassion tells us what is right. It's what enables us to truly connect with others on a deeper level. While clarity and consistency help us communicate effectively, it's compassion that helps us communicate with empathy.

We often wonder whether we can really tell the truth to our co-workers in the first place. After all, haven't we all indulged in a little white lie here and there? Nevertheless, when we run into difficult situations, we are invariably better off facing the music straight away—being uncompromisingly honest when it comes to ourselves and compassionately honest when it comes to others.

While honesty is crucial in building trust, the stark, untempered truth can be unnecessarily painful—and counterproductive. Compassionate honesty means speaking the truth, but also trying to understand and even identify with the "whys" of the other person's position and perspective. It's easier to connect with people in a meaningful way when you know where they're coming from.

Communicating with clarity, consistency, and compassion isn't just a nice thing to do; it facilitates action and builds relationships—leading to increased trust, efficiency, and a competitive edge. As Weber notes, there is a hefty price for poor communication, including "low trust, a Machiavellian environment, a lack of influence over critical decisions, and a feeling that no matter how hard you try you can't really make the team work the way you'd like."[4] Members of Accountable Organizations understand the consequences of poor communication, so they're ready and willing to roll up their sleeves and do the hard work of communicating effectively and empathetically, no matter what the medium.

Another Word About E-mail

I opened this chapter talking about e-mail, a medium that has caused us to reexamine how we communicate with one another. Consider the sheer volume of e-mail we deal with every day. In 2001, Rogen International, in conjunction with Goldhaber Research Associates, completed a study of e-mail usage in the workplace. They found that, on average, employees send twenty e-mails and receive thirty e-mails daily—amounting to about two hours of work time spent on e-mail alone.[5] I wouldn't be surprised if that number has tripled by the time you read this book.

As I noted before, e-mail has allowed us to reach more people more easily than ever before. In many ways it has greatly increased workplace efficiency—all you have to do is *cc:* your department and you're covered. The problem is that the other means of communication haven't gone away. You still have to check your voicemail and you still have meetings to attend. So while e-mail may save time in other areas, it has served to increase the information overload that people face today. There is also the question of quality. We have to make sure it cuts through the clutter. And while we're enthralled with the convenience and speed of e-mail, we can't neglect our responsibility in ensuring its value as a tool for effective and empathetic communication, despite its lack of visual and auditory clues.

Therefore, consider a few important guidelines when using e-mail. First, make your messages clear and to the point, and consider how it would appear in a more formal setting. Due to the nature of the medium—the format encourages speed, not quality—e-mail brings out the worst in us as writers. Second, respect the unique properties of e-mail and their effects on your tone. For example, you may think you're being succinct and direct, but others may view your message as curt and abrasive. Third, consider your audience and remember that e-mail can be easily forwarded. Finally, know when not to e-mail. Never reply to an e-mail in anger, and don't use e-mail to convey a message that would best be delivered in person.

Communications and Personality Type

While clarity, consistency, and compassion are the fundamental guideposts for effective and wise communication, we all know that the actual process is a highly nuanced undertaking. Even though we may be working toward a common aim, we're all unique individuals, each with our own distinct personality and frame of reference. Be they subtle or unmistakable, these differences inevitably affect how we process information, how we interact. In the field of organizational psychology, much research has been done on the effect of different personality styles on communication.

A personality tool commonly used in corporations is the *Myers-Briggs Type Indicator*® (MBTI®) instrument. The MBTI instrument has its roots in the work of Swiss psychologist Carl Jung, who posited "archetypal" personalities—patterns of behavior that we, as humans, have fallen into since the beginning of time. Whether or not you put stock in psychometric testing and personality types, it's hard to dispute the notion that we all fall into certain similar patterns and behaviors.

Why is having an understanding of personality types important for effective and empathetic communication? It's important because all personality types have a preferred way of communicating, and that way may not be readily obvious to others. While many have an intuitive gift for reading people and immediately creating rapport, most of us don't. Let's say, for example, that you have a driving personality style. You think nothing of charging into an employee's office and barking out orders. As a result, the employee, whose personality type is very different from yours, recoils, wondering why you have to be so rude. True, you're likely being clear and consistent in what you're saying, but your approach and delivery throw up a roadblock to trust. Sure, you'll get obedience. But if you had just slowed down and spoken quietly, you'd have gone further toward gaining this person's buy-in and trust.

Do you know your dominant style and how it affects your ability to communicate with people who have different styles? Think about the misunderstandings and conflicts that might have been avoided with people at work, friends, and family if only you had a better understanding of personality types.

A word of caution, however: While the MBTI personality inventory and other instruments can help us navigate our personality differences, they can't completely capture the complexities of every individual. Appropriately and ethically used, these tools can help us to better understand why people behave and communicate the way they do. When we apply this understanding in our everyday interactions and communicate with clarity, consistency, and compassion, we have a head start in building trust.

Building Customer Trust Through Effective and Empathetic Communications

What about external communications, all of which constitute marketing in one form or another? Do the same guideposts apply when communicating with customers, investors, prospects, and the media?

Imagine that you're planning a campaign to introduce a new product. What are some of your immediate considerations? First, you know that your potential audience is assaulted with thousands of messages daily, so what you say must be concise and to the point. To stand out, your message must be creative and differentiated and pack a punch. But you're not looking for a one-off; you want to create a loyal customer base for your product. And that means building trust. So your messaging not only has to make noise about your product, it also has to make a promise. Customers have to be assured that your product—and by extension, your company—deserves their trust.

This approach, what I call "trust-based marketing," is key to building fruitful, long-lasting relationships with your customers.[6] "The sale merely consummates the courtship," writes former *Harvard Business Review* editor Theodore Levitt.

"Then the marriage begins. How good the marriage is depends on how well the relationship is managed by the seller."[7] This managing of the relationship is not limited to communications. Trust-based marketing informs all aspects of marketing—branding, pricing, positioning, distribution, sales, customer service, and so on. However, for this discussion, it's worthwhile to examine how clarity, consistency, and compassion assist you in creating effective and empathetic marketing communications—thus helping you to build a trust-based brand.

Clarity in Marketing Communications

With a sea of competitors, you must get clear about what it is you want to say. Tell your customers why you're different, and be clear and concise in doing it. Does that mean your message should be stripped of emotion? Not a chance. People buy from people they like, and that means connecting on an emotional level. But people also buy from people they trust, and they're more likely to trust you if they understand the exact benefits your product or service has to offer them—and why none of your competitors can touch what you're offering. Emotion sells, but marketers in Accountable Organizations realize that substance is just as important.

Nowhere is this more evident than in the self-improvement training business—in which I've had some experience (see chapter 9). Invariably, these companies lack clarity and specificity in marketing copy when it comes to the functional benefits of their product. Visit any one of these companies' Web sites and you'll see what I mean. Many do a good job of appealing to potential customers' emotions through visual imagery and client testimonials. However, the copy is often unclear—at times unbelievable—about the specific benefits to be gained by attending one of the seminars.

Granted, marketing materials for personal growth and leadership seminars perhaps are designed to have more of an emotional appeal than those for other products. And having been through many of these seminars, I have an understanding of the benefits offered. But if companies in this industry want to experience breakthrough growth—and appeal to corporate training managers—they will have to communicate something more specific than "the experience of a lifetime." Particularly with their higher price points, these companies will have to get specific as to how seminar attendees will perform better at work as a result, learn to achieve their goals, and so on.

Consistency in Marketing Communications

Is your core message steadfast, or does it change with the wind? Successful marketers consistently reinforce their product message time and again. The approach may change, but the overarching theme is the same: *You can count on us.* For example, customers can count on BMW for sophistication, cachet, top-flight engineering, and an exhilarating driving experience. Its marketing communications continuously reinforce this message.

Customers don't like to be unpleasantly surprised; they like consistency and predictability. An overflowing marketplace is not only frustrating to marketers, it's confounding to harried consumers. An established and trusted brand is reassuring; it promises a familiar experience, reducing the risk of disappointment. Consumers like variety, to be sure, but only within a context of consistency—consistent service, consistent quality, and so on. There is power in this kind of predictability, and it needs to come across in your messaging.

Related to consistency is frequency. How frequently do you communicate with your customers? Do you keep in touch in a way that not only promotes but also provides value to your audience? As a consumer, I want to know that the companies I buy from care about me. I don't want to be inundated with generic messaging—I want tailored communication that is specific to me and my needs.

I appreciate the e-mails that I receive about once a month from Amazon.com. Based on my past purchases, the company makes suggestions about products that might interest me—and most of the time it's a decent recommendation. For me, it's the right frequency and, while unmistakably promotional, the communication itself provides value in that it alerts me to new books and music that I normally might not have heard of.

Honesty in Marketing Communications

Are you communicating honestly with your customers? As a marketer, you may say that's impossible, that you're trying to play up the positives and sell your product, not reveal its short-comings. And besides, isn't all advertising slanted in favor of the company hawking the product? Valid points.

It's true that marketing copy is designed to promote—to make people interested in a product or company. But there is a line between honest promotion and deceptive spin, and Accountable Organizations stay on the right side of that divide. There is a price to pay for spinning and lies, even omitted truths. Of course, there may be a short-term price to pay for honesty, but the long-term benefits of being forthright more than compensate. Don't hide behind overblown marketing rhetoric—show true understanding and appreciation for your customers' concerns. Tell them the truth about what they're buying and you'll earn their trust.

Clarity, consistency, and honesty in customer communications are vital for building a trust-based brand. These qualities don't preclude you from striking an emotional chord with your customers. In fact, they pave the way for making deep and lasting connections with them—thus potentially reducing the cost of retaining them.

Communication During a Crisis: Tylenol® and Tires

Of course, the true test of effective and empathetic communication comes with crisis. How companies react when their feet are held to the fire stays with consumers for a long, long time. In terms of trust, it can make a company—or break it.

Consider the quintessential case study of Johnson & Johnson and the Tylenol® crisis. In the 1980s, unknown individuals laced Tylenol capsules with cyanide, resulting in several deaths. Johnson & Johnson didn't equivocate; it immediately announced the situation publicly and recalled the product. As the investigation continued (no one was ever convicted for the tampering and resulting deaths), company officials consistently and frequently kept the public informed.

It's clear that Johnson & Johnson's communication during the tampering crisis—backed by action and results—saved the Tylenol brand and reinforced the company's reputation as a "guardian of the public health."[8] After its reintroduction, Tylenol ultimately reclaimed leadership of the analgesic market. Furthermore, Johnson & Johnson became a pioneer of tamper-resistant packaging, an innovation that would be adopted industrywide and beyond.

Contrast the Tylenol case with the more recent crisis involving Bridgestone/Firestone, Inc., and Ford Motor Company. Tread separation led to hundreds of fatal accidents involving Bridgestone tires on Ford Explorers. Under tremendous pressure Bridgestone recalled 6.5 million tires in August 2000. The two companies engaged in a very public blame game; amid climbing death tolls, media coverage portrayed Bridgestone and Ford as being more concerned with protecting themselves than with protecting their customers.

Ford claimed the deaths were due to faulty tires, while Bridgestone said a design flaw of the Explorer shared in the blame. After a long-entwined history dating back to the friendship between their respective founders, Bridgestone and Ford acrimoniously severed their ties. Both brands suffered—as of this writing, Bridgestone still hasn't recovered from the impact of its handling of the issue. Ford lost ground in both SUV market share and in consumer surveys.

One of those surveys was the Harris Interactive annual ranking of corporate reputations. In 2002, more than twenty-two thousand people rated sixty companies on six key dimensions: products and services, financial performance, workplace environment, social responsibility, vision and leadership, and emotional appeal. Ford was the lowest-ranked auto company, placing forty-third overall (an improvement over its 2001 ranking of fifty-second). Bridgestone/Firestone placed a dismal fifty-fifth overall, after finishing dead last in 2001.

In contrast, Johnson & Johnson ranked number one—for the fourth year in a row.

"Johnson & Johnson has just always been a very trust-worthy company," one Missouri woman told the *Wall Street Journal.* "Their ads are honest. They don't talk down to me. They think consumers have brains." Meanwhile, a man who experienced a Firestone tire blowout told the paper: "Firestone seems to have finally admitted the problem. Now it's up to [them] to tell it straight: What did you do to correct the situation? We consumers aren't tire engineers, but we know BS when it's offered."[9]

About ten years ago I was involved in a serious car accident in which my Ford Explorer literally saved my life. Based on my own personal experience, I trusted in the safety of Ford

Explorers—and, given the SUV's popularity, so did thousands of other consumers. Similarly, in the years before the tampering incident, most consumers believed Tylenol was one of the safest drugs on the market. Postcrisis, Tylenol upheld, even enhanced, its brand image. As of now, Firestone, and to a degree, Ford, have not. A large part of the difference was in the quality of each company's communication to the public. How these organizations communicated with their customers likely played a large part in their decisions about whether to remain customers—or take their business elsewhere.

Building Trust, Resolving Conflict

In summary, effective and empathetic communication is one of the most powerful ways to build trust. It's the primary tool for connecting with an audience, for letting them know that you are accountable as a company, an executive, an employee. The rules are simple: look your audience in the eye and be clear, consistent, and compassionate. Your authenticity will pay dividends—you'll build trust with your customers, helping your bottom line. And within the organization, you'll increase team cohesion and productivity. As we'll see in chapter 8, effective and empathetic communication is vital in confronting and resolving conflict.

BUILDING THE
ACCOUNTABLE ORGANIZATION

1. Overall, how would you rate your organization's internal communication in terms of clarity, consistency, and compassion? Consider instances in which better communication could have resulted in a better outcome or even averted a crisis. What mechanisms and/or changes in philosophy could be instituted to improve performance in these areas?

2. Review your external communications with customers and your marketing materials. Evaluate these communications in terms of clarity, consistency, and compassion and devise strategies for improving performance in these areas. Examine previous breakdowns in communication with customers and identify where better choices could have been made.

3. How would you rate your own communication when it comes to clarity, consistency, and compassion? Can you think of any episodes in which better communication would have helped you avoid conflict? How will you commit to improving your performance in these areas?

CHAPTER EIGHT

CONFLICT
Seeking Resolution Through Preparation and Negotiation

In ten years of marriage and twenty in business, I've learned much about conflict—how I identify it, how I approach dealing with it. I now know that conflict is something to be appreciated. At the risk of oversimplifying my position to "no pain, no gain," it is indeed by managing through dilemmas, uncomfortable conversations, and day-to-day conflict that we become stronger, wiser, and more compassionate. Where there is conflict, there is opportunity.

Why Bother with Conflict?

It goes without saying that people face conflict in the workplace every day. The issue may be between co-workers, a subordinate and a supervisor, a salesperson and a customer, a production line worker and a crew manager, and so on. The conflict could be between people, groups, or some combination thereof. We will always have conflict because each of us has our own view of how the world works and what we want. The question isn't whether there will be conflict; it's what to do with it when it surfaces.

Perhaps you will identify with the following situations. They are common examples of conflict—or at least potential conflict—brewing in the workplace.

- Your star performer is disruptive in company meetings, making inappropriate jokes that sometimes insult others in the group. Despite continued warnings and coaching from you, his behavior continues. What do you do?

- An employee has just received a performance review that, from the employee's perspective, is unfair. Should the employee raise the issue with her supervisor, whom she believes to be single-minded and short-tempered?

- You've just moved to a new office and your colleague in the office next to yours is a chatterbox, constantly interrupting your work. How do you approach the issue, knowing that if you don't, your performance will suffer?

- Management has just issued a wage freeze in response to poor company performance. Only weeks earlier, you had been told that you will be getting a raise. Should you confront your supervisor and ask if your raise would still be granted?

- Two of your best employees have begun a romantic relationship outside the office. You are concerned about future implications to your business, no matter how the office romance turns out. How do you approach this problem?

There isn't a silver bullet for dealing with all the complex situations businesses and people face. Conflict resolution falls into that category of desperately needed life skills—such as marriage and parenting—that we don't learn in school. But similar to managing your relationships or raising children, conflict resolution is a discipline to be practiced, refined, and challenged throughout a lifetime. The good news is that there are tools available to use when you find yourself in the middle of a difficult situation—and pitfalls to watch out for before you engage.

Why Conflict Is Difficult to Face

Our individual upbringing and experience have influenced each of us differently in terms of how we view conflict. Craig Weber says conflict generally produces one of two responses in people: engage or avoid.

Basically, when there's a tough issue to confront—when there's a tough conversation to address, when someone's doing something we don't like—we revert to some fairly primal mental reactions. One is to get away from it, and we often will get away from it by either physically leaving or by avoiding the conversation with that person because we don't want to make it worse—we don't want to escalate the problem. Very often we do a quick calculus in our head that says, if I engage with this person, it might get ugly and nasty and I may look bad, and if I don't engage the issue, it probably won't go away. Sometimes we just decide to play it safe and live with the problem. On the other hand, some of us do the calculus and think, I don't care if I look bad, I don't care if this person gets upset. What's important to me is swaying the way they look at the problem. It's getting my point across. From this position, we can be very argumentative, we can get very positional . . . we can get outright condescending.[1]

As Weber says, whether we choose to engage or to avoid often depends on our own in-the-moment cost-benefit analysis of the implications. If I confront the problem, will there be some damage to my relationship with this person? If I avoid or ignore the problem, is it likely to get worse? Unfortunately, in many conflicted situations—such as the scenarios above—both outcomes are likely possible. If you are confrontational, something bad might come out of it, particularly if you don't approach it in the right way (although some people don't care—they just want to get their way and be right). And we know intuitively that left alone, problems don't go away; they rumble like shifting plates in the earth until a full-blown earthquake strikes.

Douglas Stone, Bruce Patton, and Sheila Heen of the Harvard Negotiation Project recognize the inherent challenge of managing the kinds of "difficult conversations" involved in confronting conflict.

> *Delivering a difficult message is like throwing a hand grenade. Coated with sugar, thrown hard or soft, a hand grenade is still going to do damage. Try as you may, there's no way to throw a hand grenade with tact or to outrun the circumstances. And keeping it to yourself is no better. Choosing not to deliver a difficult message is like hanging onto a hand grenade after you've pulled the pin. Because at some level we know the truth: If we try to avoid the problem, we'll feel taken advantage of, our feelings will fester, we'll wonder why we don't stick up for ourselves, and we'll rob the other person of the opportunity to improve things. But if we confront the problem, things might get even worse. We may be rejected or attacked; we might hurt the other person in ways we didn't intend; and the relationship might suffer.*[2]

So, in some ways it may seem that we're damned if we do, damned if we don't. There may not be a clear solution in sight. Nonetheless, in Accountable Organizations it's imperative to tackle conflict, to face the difficult conversations. To see why, let's take a look at conflict from the perspective of integrity, accountability, and trust.

- **Integrity.** If the conflict is serious enough—and if you're going through all the mental machinations, it probably is—your values and beliefs are at stake. If you ignore the conflict and let the problem ride, your personal integrity might take a blow. Remember, part of integrity is standing up for what's right, even in the face of adversity.

- **Accountability.** In conflicts between two people, both sides are usually contributing somehow to the disagreement. In claiming accountability, you must acknowledge your role in getting into this mess in the first place. This is the hardest part to recognize, since you may be thinking it's all the other person's fault.

- **Trust.** Members of Accountable Organizations seek to create trust internally (with colleagues, subordinates, and supervisors) and externally (with shareholders, customers, the media, and so on). If you have a conflict that isn't being addressed, trust between the parties is taking a beating. If you are successful in managing through the conflict, trust is earned on both sides.

Getting Prepared

Your approach to conflict resolution can largely determine the outcome. For this reason preparation, with an eye toward understanding both sides of the issue, is key. William Ury, co-founder of the Program on Negotiation at Harvard University, stresses the importance of preparation for negotiation and conflict resolution.

> *Most negotiations are won or lost even before the talking begins, depending upon the quality of the presentation. People who think they can "wing it" without preparing often find themselves sadly mistaken. Even if they reach agreement, they may miss opportunities for joint gain they might well have come across in preparing. There is no substitute for effective preparation. The more difficult the negotiation, the more intensive your preparation needs to be.*[3]

Before you address any conflict, you need as much information as possible. You need to know what is true and what information is missing. You need to be keenly aware of your worldview and how it influences your perspective on the situation, what psychologists call "cognitive bias." You need to understand your emotions and how they are affecting your decisions. In addition, you should know the other person's position on these points, as well. Try to empathize with the other person. How would *she* describe the problem and the history of what's going on between you? What are *her* cognitive biases, as best you can predict? How is she likely to be feeling? However unattractive the prospect may seem at the time, it's crucial to make an honest attempt at seeing the conflict from the other person's perspective.

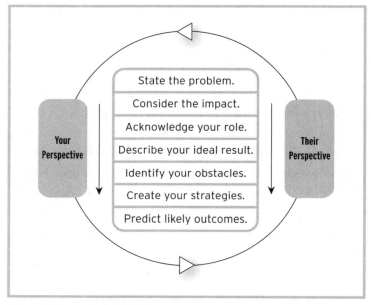

Figure 1: Assessing Conflict

Creating an Action Plan for Addressing Conflict

When I'm facing a serious conflict, I create an action plan for resolving it, as I do for any difficult problem I'm facing (see fig. 1). You may have your own process. What's important is to take the time in advance to work it through.

1. **State the problem.** In the clearest terms possible, I describe the problem, who is involved, and why—and make sure it's not just a symptom of a larger problem.

I think through the history—all that has happened to lead me to this pivotal place. What events have played a role in this conflict?

2. **Consider the impact.** I then look to see how the conflict is affecting my business, my personal relationships, or other areas of my life. What is the financial (and social) impact on my business? If I don't deal with the conflict, what do I project will happen?

3. **Acknowledge your role.** What role have I been playing in the conflict thus far? This is the most challenging part of the exercise, because it forces me to identify my own accountability in a situation in which I believe I'm "right." (And I very well may be.)

4. **Describe your ideal result.** I try to be clear about what I want. In the best of all worlds, if I were to successfully work through the conflict, what would my best result look like? After going through the steps above, I sometimes have a different result in mind than when I started.

5. **Identify your obstacles.** What's getting in the way of resolving this conflict? The biggest barrier to getting past the conflict may be *me*. I also look at it from others' points of view, and what their barriers might be.

6. **Create your strategies.** I identify strategies for confronting and overcoming the barriers that stand in the way of resolving the conflict.

7. **Predict likely outcomes.** In advance, I identify the likely outcomes of confronting the conflict, including worst- and best-case scenarios, as well as some in between.

I find it helpful in this kind of exercise to repeatedly ask the quintessential journalist's question, *Why?* Why is this a problem in the first place? Why have I contributed to the problem? Why is this the result that I want? The more times I ask why, the better I understand the true issue at hand.

Addressing the Other Side

Once you have prepared yourself, it's time to address the other person, or persons, involved. Sometimes, if it's a particularly challenging issue, it may be helpful to script out the conversation in advance. And always, if at all possible, meet in person—if necessary, in a moderated environment. In an ideal world, the conversation would progress as follows:

1. **State the situation as you see it.** Calmly share with the other person your perspective on what is going wrong and the history behind it, including the facts (as you believe them to be) and what is at stake. Acknowledge that this is *your* perspective on the situation, and, if possible, offer your best, most respectful description of what you believe to be her perspective. Talk through what you see to be getting in the way of resolution, but refrain from suggesting solutions early in the conversation.

2. **Be accountable for your role in the situation.** Even if you believe you are in the right, you've likely had some role in letting the conflict reach the point that it has. For example, perhaps you could have approached the other person sooner. Facilitate the other person's acceptance of his accountability by setting the example.

3. **Get feedback.** Ask the other person to describe the situation and its history from her perspective—what she believes to be the facts and the issues at stake. Be calm and open-minded; if not empathetic, at least try to be compassionate and understanding.

4. **Mutually decide on a resolution.** Having stated your case, take turns with the other person in describing how you would like to see the situation resolved. Show your commitment to reaching a compromise and work with the other person to reach a solution that satisfies you both.

Of course, it would be wonderful if these steps would work without fail, that after it all you'd both head off for coffee, laughing and wondering why you ever argued in the first place. In an ideal world, all conflicts would be resolved so easily. But despite our best efforts to be calm and rational, the fact is that emotion is inherent in conflict. That's not to say that there isn't any value in doing your best to follow the steps outlined above. In fact, they've helped me to better resolve many conflicts both at my company and at home.

But all too often, someone throws you a curveball during the process and all bets are off. I remember one situation involving a conflict with a friend. I did all my homework. I identified the problem and its history, knew the stakes, accepted full responsibility for my role, and had my ideal resolution in mind. My friend and I agreed to meet, one-on-one. All systems go. Ten minutes into the conversation, however, I was shouting at my friend (and I'm not even the yelling type), who in turn stormed out of my office. This person was flat-out refusing to get past our issues, refused to accept accountability, and, damn it, I wouldn't stand for it! How quickly our emotions can get the better of us.

Frankly, there is no fool-proof prescription for conflict resolution.[4] The best you can do is thoroughly prepare yourself and truly commit to working toward a solution that serves the interests of all parties as much as possible. Use the steps above to help keep you on track.

And what if you still find yourself at an impasse? Well, unfortunately, the truth is that not all conflicts can be settled. There are times when people, and organizations, can't come to a mutual agreement that satisfies the win-win objective. Some intraorganizational disputes are intractable; or, at the very least, one conversation isn't going to be sufficient to resolve the situation. When you find yourself in these kinds of situations, it's easy to feel trapped. However, you can strive to look beyond the obvious and not disavow the ownership you have over your choices. Some of the options may not be desirable, but you still have the power to decide. The one choice you shouldn't make, however, is to wallow in the situation, to remain stuck at the impasse. Decide for yourself whether there is a creative solution you can commit to, or if you should simply move on. At some point we all have to choose our battles.

Dealing with Organizational Conflict: An Example from FWI

Earlier in this book I described a situation at FWI in which many of us, myself included, relinquished accountability. We all denied the roles we had in either creating the situation or impeding its resolution. Communication shut down, resulting in an atmosphere of distrust and anger. I called a meeting to address the issue, but no one would engage in discussion. People refused to speak their mind about the issues involved, no matter how much I prodded and pleaded.

What I wanted to hear from the people in my organization was their honest assessment of what they were experiencing, what they felt was at the root of the problem, and how they would like to see it resolved. As we had done in the past with other challenging issues, I thought we could approach the issue logically, going through the steps and collectively reaching a decision. But that didn't happen. So I went back to the drawing board and once again asked, "Why?" An important piece was missing—something was keeping people from claiming their accountability in the situation and moving forward to a solution.

I realized that the problem really came down to trust. Before, the inherent tension between sales and editorial/production had always been mitigated by trust. When that trust is lost, however, competition overpowers cooperation. The problem had run so deep and for so long that neither side trusted the other—and what's worse, there was little trust in management to solve the problem.

We see a similar dynamic in organizations with unions, particularly with multiple unions, as in the airline industry. The pilots want something (usually more money and job security), the flight attendants want something (the same thing), the aircraft mechanics want something (ditto), and they all know they can't have it all at the same time. And many of them don't trust management, who they may see as wanting to keep wages low and profits high to fill the company coffers and pad executive bonuses. In these cases, negotiations often seem doomed before they begin.

When it came to the situation at FWI, the distrust made my employees unwilling to communicate. Distrust breeds fear—for example, fear of looking foolish, or fear of possible retribution. It was enough to keep them silent. And that was a huge problem for me as CEO. After all, aside from the role I played in this particular problem, my larger responsibility as a leader is to set the context—to create an environment of trust and communication. And that meant the first person they needed to trust and communicate with was me.

Taking the first step toward resolution, I first looked at my own role in the situation—first from the perspective of a person who seeks to be accountable in his relationships with others. I ran through the exercise: How had I ducked out on the people who needed my guidance and support, and why? Then, I looked at my role within the larger responsibility I had as CEO. How had I fallen short? Why had I pushed off the management problem on the general manager? What structures needed to be changed within the organization in order to facilitate communication? In my mind, I was clear about my objective: to move our company out of the funk and back to a trusting—and fully accountable—environment.

Next, I looked at the problem from the perspective of the other parties involved:

- The production and editorial staffs were angry and resentful toward the sales and marketing group for not pitching in to help and having no empathy. Furthermore, they had lost trust and confidence that management cared about the issue and was interested in a solution.

- The sales and marketing group didn't see any problem at all since it was their job to bring in business—so what if it meant the editorial and production staff were overworked? It was a "good" problem to have.

- The editorial chief felt powerless to fix the situation, had lost confidence in me, and was angry with the GM.

- In turn, the GM considered the editorial and production staff to be complaining about what was a short-term problem, and he protected the sales group's right to sell as much as possible, no matter how it was impacting the lives of everyone else.

I held another meeting, but one I felt was better designed to alleviate fear and regain trust. I went directly to the editorial staff, alone. I sat among them in their space. I shared my observations about the previous meeting, and how I was concerned that no one felt comfortable enough to speak their mind. Next, I took full accountability for my role in the process.

I let everyone know that I wanted to effect change, but I couldn't do it in a vacuum. I needed their help, which meant their giving me their honest assessments of the problems they faced and potential solutions. Finally, and most important, I told the group that what we discussed would be confidential, that I would do my best to be an impartial listener, and that no one need fear retribution. It was a long meeting. It wasn't easy getting things started; people still felt a bit ill at ease, but eventually the problems, concerns, and feelings began to percolate to the surface.

I believe the three things that were most important in putting them at ease were (1) choice of venue; (2) acknowledging my role in the conflict; and (3) showing a genuine desire to hear them out. More than anything, the team simply wanted to know that management—me in particular—was taking their issues and concerns seriously. They had had this chance before, yes, but they didn't feel safe in putting themselves on the line. Now, they were sufficiently reassured, and the words began to flow. And within thirty minutes, the group was suggesting ideas for moving past the situation.

This was only the first step. After my meeting with the editorial staff, more conversations, and further reflection, I understood that this conflict had revealed a larger problem within the organization: the *system* for supporting accountability needed to be changed. It led to a restructuring of our company, one in which a new management team would have cooperative responsibility across all areas of the business. The team developed a cross-functional communication plan that allowed for improved resource planning. In other words, everyone would be armed with better and more frequent information, have a deeper understanding of each department's needs, and experience better advocacy at the managerial level.

Changing the structure was done with specific intentions: to improve communication and managerial effectiveness, and to set the stage for increased trust. I'm not depending solely on the structure, however, to ensure that these things happen. People are responsible for the success of an organization, and certainly the team I have in place is charged with these things. As am I.

From Risk Comes Opportunity

Conflict resolution is an ongoing process—unlike in movies and sitcoms, there is rarely one moment in which all disagreements are neatly settled to everyone's satisfaction. However, that doesn't mean that the members of an organization shouldn't strive to settle the conflicts they have with one another. It may not happen overnight, but with determination and dedication, it can happen. Thomas Crum observes,

"Resolving conflict is rarely about who is right. It is about acknowledgement and appreciation of differences."[5]

The rewards of this acknowledgment and appreciation can be great. "Some conflict is productive and necessary for an effective organization, as constructive use of differences fosters organizational excellence," note authors Kirk Blackard and James Gibson. They stress that conflict—when properly managed—can boost creativity in an organization through healthy interchange, improve decisions by having different viewpoints, and contribute to organizational learning.[6]

Of course, it can be difficult to see the potential for opportunity within conflict. One of the daunting realizations about conflict is that there may not be a clear solution in sight—in other words, there is risk involved in taking that first conciliatory step. However, unless we're willing to take a risk, we'll never discover the opportunities that lie beyond the horizon.

BUILDING THE
ACCOUNTABLE ORGANIZATION

1. How effective are the people within your organization— including yourself—in taking on conflict? What kinds of cultural, or even physical, obstacles exist to confronting and resolving conflict? What kinds of strategies can your organization employ to improve conflict resolution?

2. Think of a conflict you were involved in that ended badly or one that is currently brewing between you and another individual. Assess this conflict using the seven steps outlined in this chapter (see pp. 126–128).

3. If the conflict has passed, consider how preparing yourself in this manner might have resulted in a better outcome and, if feasible, revisit the issue with the other party involved (and rewrite history). If the conflict is current, use this information to confront and resolve the issue.

CHAPTER NINE

RISK
Breaking Barriers Creatively and Courageously

Sometimes the prospect of risk can be daunting, particularly in uncertain times. As the U.S. economy continued to slouch through winter 2003, *BusinessWeek* senior writer John A. Byrne pointed to low confidence in CEOs as one of the many factors conspiring to keep American business in the doldrums. "Not all that long ago, with soaring stock prices and labor shortages, CEOs were almost cultural icons," Byrne observed. "Today, with the combination of a weak economy, an ever-lower stock market, and a startling succession of corporate scandals, they're embattled, belittled, and cursed."[1]

The Role of Risk in Accountable Organizations

According to Byrne, CEOs across the board are paying for the sins of the few. The overwhelming public disdain, coupled with weak earnings and shaky consumer confidence, is not encouraging business leaders to take risks. Instead, they're homing in on cutting costs. Jeffrey E. Garten, author and dean of the Yale School of Management, says it's understandable that uncertainty drives leaders to circle the wagons and focus solely on execution. However, he goes on to caution that

> *execution alone will not lead U.S. industry out of its funk. We can all agree that having a vision without the ability to carry it out is no more than wishful thinking. But the opposite is no better. What good is execution if the strategy and goals are the wrong ones? In fact, the emerging virus in American business culture could be the penchant for playing it too safe—settling for nothing more than getting things done and gearing everything to meeting quarterly targets, while failing to exercise enough imagination about where to go and what to be.[2]*

Furthermore, chief executives shouldn't forget that smart risk taking is in their job description. "Dynamic capitalism isn't just about cutting costs or staying afloat," Garten writes. "It's about thinking of how to make the future better and placing bets on that vision."[3] Indeed, leaders within Accountable Organizations must embrace risk as a necessary part of what they do. Otherwise, they may be trading in their company's future for an increased sense of security in the present. That security may be fleeting if the company isn't ready for new opportunities. In fact, we as consumers *expect* companies to take risks. We're always asking, "What's next?" We expect companies to be a few steps ahead of us with the answer.

Profits are the lifeblood ensuring that an Accountable Organization endures and grows, that it will be around to make a difference in stakeholders' lives. And taking risks—educated, responsible risks—is necessary for an Accountable Organization to innovate and compete, to achieve and sustain profitability. Three concepts underlie this kind of risk taking:

1. **Creativity.** While corporate scandals have added an unsavory angle to the concept of creativity (e.g., "creative accounting" has become a common phrase), it's truly the stuff of our imagination that fuels our economy. It's the ability to imagine the possibilities—and the freedom to pursue and realize those possibilities—that motivates us to endeavor. In order for us to take a risk in the first place, we must have an idea upon which we're "placing our bets."

2. **Courage.** Creativity means nothing when there's no will to implement it. Organizations and stakeholders that wish to succeed must find the mettle within to make the leap. This can be especially difficult during uncertain times. Of course, it is during uncertain times when courage is most in need.

3. **Conscientiousness.** The courage to take risks should not be misplaced, however. Accountability means that risk cannot

be taken without due diligence, without an honest audit of the foreseeable consequences, which includes identifying potential benefits . . . and potential casualties. The possibility of failure is inherent in risk, and risk takers in Accountable Organizations do their best to weigh the costs of that possibility against the likelihood of success.

During the heady days of the late 1990s, there was no shortage of creativity and courage—some would say audacity—when it came to risk taking. In the euphoria, conscientiousness seemed outdated. Now that the gold rush is over and reality has set in, some may be taking conscientiousness to the extreme, deeming any risk unacceptable. As Byrne and Garten rightly point out, this kind of thinking won't propel business out of its slump. Now is the time for educated, responsible risk taking—by both the leaders *and* stakeholders in Accountable Organizations.

Risk and the Executive

While those at the highest levels of an organization can have the most impact by taking risks—they have the broadest scope when it comes to decision making—they may not always be inclined to do so, weak economy aside. Perhaps they have worked all their life to achieve their position and are happy to plant their lawn chair on top of the mountain. The last thing they want to do is risk what they worked so hard to earn.

Yet wouldn't you rather be the CEO who led your company to record sales and profitability? Or would you prefer to maintain the status quo, only to be replaced and watch your successor, a so-called turnaround artist, take all the credit? (Of course, turnaround artists may have it easier, as they have more permission to be muckrakers.) Working hard to get to the top is admirable. But once you're there, it's your responsibility to keep the organization healthy and primed for the future. As a leader, you must fight complacency and continue to push the envelope. Your company depends on it.

Like many entrepreneurs, I'm comfortable with risk. I took a risk in starting my company. I take a risk every time I give the go-ahead for a new product or hire a new employee, particularly if the product requires great investment or the person comes with a high price tag. The way I see it, it's riskier *not* to launch new products or hire top talent. FWI, like virtually all companies interested in survival and prosperity, is dependent on growth—and the only way to grow is to take risks. Products that are relevant today may go the way of the dinosaurs within a few short years, even months. To stay ahead of the curve, businesses—and the people who lead them—must embrace risk.

My rule of thumb for the CEO of a large, established company is to strive to grow the business between 10 and 15 percent each year, both gross and net. If you lead a medium- to small-sized firm, double that goal. And if you're an entrepreneur in the early stages of the game, double it again. It's your job to identify the opportunities that will get you to that level of growth. How are you going to post numbers like that if you don't take risks? (Note: I am not suggesting growth for the sake

of growth. I use these guidelines as a reminder to keep push-
ing the business forward, and the clearest indicator you have
is financial performance. But temper that desire for growth
with realistic expectations of where a company is in its growth
cycle, the conditions of the market, the industry, and so on.
Expecting a Wal-Mart, for example, to grow at 15 percent
annually is unrealistic—and could lead to the same kinds of
problems that we found in companies pursuing growth at any
cost in the 1990s.)

At my company, it's only natural that the greatest
gambles—those with the biggest potential payoffs—come
from me. Nonetheless, my employees know that FWI's culture is one in which their own risk taking is encouraged and
rewarded. Of course, there are those who are more at ease taking risks than others, so part of my role is to encourage everyone to stretch beyond their own individual comfort zones, to
do things differently.

To get the stakeholder perspective, I asked people from
FWI's editorial, operations, finance, and sales areas to describe
the ideal organizational environment for encouraging risk.
Here's what some of them said:

> **Editorial.** *"Personally, I think it is feeling that I will be
> rewarded for original thought and for taking my ideas to the
> people who can use them. Sometimes, of course, I don't know
> that my ideas are good ones, which makes it a risk to come
> out with them. Nonetheless, I feel rewarded for, if nothing
> else, trying to be innovative. Even when people have innova-*

tive ideas that, to be honest, are stupid, the fact that they are brave enough to throw it out there is appreciated because . . . how else is the company going to evolve and improve?"

Operations. "As clichéd as the terminology has become, 'ouside-the-box' thinking should be highly regarded. Those who don't run with an idea or seek tasks outside their normal duties do not move up the totem pole. Additionally, when a person takes a risk and does not achieve her goal, the attempt is not looked down upon but instead is considered a learning experience. I do consider myself a risk taker, especially when it comes to voicing my ideas for ways to improve aspects of the business. While not all my ideas have worked, many have been implemented and did indeed improve various processes. I cannot help by staying quiet when I see that something can be done better, more quickly, or more efficiently."

Sales. "Risk should be rewarded. In my own situation, I definitely take risks with my clients, but they are ethical risks. Some of the business that I have brought in has required imagination and stretching on everybody's part. As a result of these risks, the company has grown and evolved a little bit more, and that is very rewarding for me . . . It makes my job challenging and fun."

These comments show that maintaining a culture in which risk taking is supported requires continuous reinforcement from the leadership. As CEO, I can't simply proclaim that risk taking within the company is expected and then leave it at that. Similar to my responsibility concerning communication and conflict resolution, I must work to cultivate an atmosphere in which stakeholders feel safe putting themselves out there. And ultimately, that means working to increase trust.

Of course, if someone is just severely risk averse, all the training in the world won't change that outlook. At the other end of the spectrum, there are people who fearlessly go to the wall for their ideas. However, it can be very hard to find the latter individuals for your team; and if you have them, you might need to make sure they are conscientious in their risk taking. Most leaders will find that the majority of their people are on the fence when it comes to risk—they may just need a little encouragement to make the leap. Build trust and spread the passion about what your company does and you'll encourage people to put themselves on the line and take their performance—and the company's—to the next level.

Risk and the Employee

No matter your place in the organizational hierarchy, do you embrace risk as an essential part of your contribution to the company? Or are you comfortable in your position, happy to let someone else bear the burden of risk? It's interesting—people often talk about starting their own business but then don't because they say the risks are too great. When pressed, these individuals may say they're afraid of losing money. In my opinion, I think they're more afraid that their risk may end in failure. As we all know, however, working for someone else doesn't insulate you from failure. In fact, when we sit back and let someone else take the reins, we may think we absolve ourselves of risk, when in fact we're engaging in the riskiest behavior of all: giving up control over our own destiny.

I'll admit, I've indulged in that kind of thinking. At my former company, my colleagues and I would refer to "the chessboard." We often felt we were at the mercy of the machinations of upper management. But I was wrong—far from being some inert pawn, I had full control over the quality of my work and the strength of my relationships throughout the organization. In fact, I had enormous influence on how management viewed me, and could create opportunities for myself—if only I took ownership of that power. For example, let's say that an important position was being created to oversee a new product. The rulers of the chessboard would sit down and ask, Who has been creating the greatest results in our organization? Who not only has the experience but also the drive to make this product a success? Who is connected and knows how to manage relationships with others within the organization? Who is smart and dynamic? Who is a proven leader?

During my last year with that company, my wife gave me a framed picture of a large sailboat heading out to sea. Entitled "Risk," it was one of those popular motivational posters that peppered the halls of corporate America at the time. The caption underneath the picture read: "You cannot discover new oceans unless you have the courage to lose sight of the shore." Every day I went to work and looked at the poster—it was a constant motivation to me as I contemplated starting my own company. But its meaning was the same for me as for a stake-holder in a large corporation.

There are plenty of opportunities within the corporate culture for taking risks, be they large or small—approaching a problem in a new way, taking that innovative idea and giving it life . . . making your own destiny by being creative, courageous, and conscientious to the best of your ability and to the greatest extent possible within your environment. The path won't necessarily be easy: there will be ideas that don't work, roadblocks to execution, resistant managers who are themselves threatened by risk taking. But if you persevere, odds are that you will differentiate yourself—and make a difference in the process. Perhaps you will inspire your colleagues to take some risks; maybe one will get up the nerve to propose that idea he has been silently harboring. At my former company, my most memorable achievements resulted from projects in which I took a significant risk. Spread the word, lead by example.

No matter what business you're in, as an employee-stakeholder you have signed on to participate in a collective endeavor of creativity. In a rapidly evolving marketplace, companies must continuously innovate to keep providing value for their customers, both external and internal. You have a vital role in this process: it entails realizing how your own creativity and initiative can make a difference, and doing something about it. Don't discount your importance—stand up and make that difference.

When Taking a Risk Ends in Failure

Earlier in this book, I touched on a difficult period I experienced during the early days of FWI. I was raising questions about the meaning and truth in everything, including who I was and what I was to become. Obviously, this is not a unique experience. These kinds of questions surface for all of us as we wrestle with our humanity, wondering what's the point . . . or even if there is a point at all.

But let me back up a little. Ever since my youth I've been intrigued by the concept of personal excellence—the science and art behind human potential. It may sound odd, but as a teenager I loved listening to motivational speaking tapes I'd borrowed from my dad. I would play these recordings again and again, fascinated by the stories of greatness and intrigued by the secrets of excellence. This interest continued throughout college, graduate school, and beyond. And when I later found myself questioning everything, I turned to seminar training, driven in great part by my desire to find the key to what makes a person successful—or at least the commonalities among successful people.

I took courses in leadership, entrepreneurship, and negotiations. And my search for answers had an unintended side effect: as I was studying, I often pictured myself in front of the room—as the teacher instead of the student. Years before, I had taught several marketing classes at the local community college. Now that I was back in a learning environment, I found myself missing that experience, that interaction with curious learners. It was about that time that my business mentor approached me about becoming an executive coach. Intrigued, I headed off to a three-week training program run by a California-based company. The program not only taught me invaluable coaching skills, it also inspired me to go down the path of serious introspection. For me, it was the right place at the right moment.

Though I didn't stay in the executive coaching field for long—the demands were too great at a time when FWI needed my full attention—I kept in close contact with the training company. Two years later, through an odd chain of events, the company's leaders approached me with an interesting proposition.

The founder, whom I'll call Dave, had been having problems. While his consulting practice was thriving, his seminar product line was languishing. The shoestring sales staff was barely keeping it alive, and its losses were eating into the profits of the consulting business. Dave flew to Phoenix and proposed that he spin off the bleeding seminar business to me. I was hesitant, but agreed to take a look.

Considering my interest in personal excellence, the vehicle was perfect. While I had some issues concerning the structure of the seminars themselves, I believed that the main problem lay with how they were marketed. I decided to take the risk. I agreed, in principle, to take this dying product and breathe life into it. I thought it was just a matter of strategy, money, and time before we would have rooms full of eager, paying customers. Moreover, I would finally have the opportunity to teach others what I believed about success and personal excellence. I had the means to the end.

This will give you some insight into my perspective on risk: even before we had a deal in place, I incorporated the seminar line as a new business and hired four people. I had a close relationship with Dave and wanted to hit the ground running. I mean, how hard could the seminar business be? (If you run a seminar business, you might as well skip the next few sentences. You probably already know how the story ends.) Well, I'll tell you how hard it is. We worked day and night to get the business off the ground. We gave away seats to fill the rooms. After five months with only $9,500 in revenue, I realized that it just wouldn't be possible financially to make this new company work. After much agonizing, I shut down the business and returned everything to Dave. Amazingly, even after five months, we still didn't have a signed partnership deal. We had never come to terms about what our partnership would look like, and now it was over.

Lessons Learned

On one hand, this experience was a lesson to me in the importance of conscientiousness when it comes to risk taking. Before taking over the seminar business, I set limits concerning the amount of money and time I'd devote to this new venture. When I exceeded the money limit long before the time limit, I knew it was time to pull the plug, even though it hurt to do so. But should I have even entered into this arrangement in the first place? Because of my risk-taking nature, I'm inclined to jump head first into interesting challenges—in this case, so much so that I refused to be dissuaded by others who could judge the situation much more objectively. Looking back, I had tepid support from stakeholders at FWI, who were rightly concerned about me stretching myself too thin. Similarly, when I proposed the idea to my fellow members of TEC, a peer-group organization for CEOs, the response was unanimous: Don't do it. I went ahead anyway, and the failure, though costly, wasn't fatal. The experience taught me that in the future, my passion and propensity for risk must be tempered with a bit more due diligence.

That being said, the experience itself also taught me a lesson about accountability and integrity. Aside from my self-imposed financial limitations, Dave and I never finalized our business partnership because we ran into larger issues of values and beliefs. Having founded the seminar business, Dave obviously had very specific ideas of what they should be. At first, I concurred with his vision. However, after months of analysis, brand work, and product development, I discovered that I had a very different vision for the seminars. Like Dave, I had been studying the issues surrounding personal excellence for twenty years. But we had come to different conclusions about how to guide others in their own pursuit of it. This became clear only after months of intense meetings, philosophical discussions, and collaborative analysis. In the end, we found that neither of us could follow the other's path, not for all the money in the world.

Because both of us took full ownership of our roles in the relationship, we were able to amicably part company. Was there disappointment and frustration? Absolutely. But because we stood by our beliefs—yet were respectful of each other's position—we were able to salvage our relationship from the failed partnership. Thus, the experience reinforced the value of accountability and integrity both in business and in life.

The Final Lesson

And finally, the experience reinforced for me a vital lesson about the nature of success, one that I first learned back when I was sixteen, surreptitiously listening to my father's motivational tapes. It's a common theme, but one that we often forget in our winner-take-all culture: Success is an ongoing process, a path rather than a final destination. And risk taking is a vital part of that process, as important as hard work. The worthiness of our goals, principles, and dreams inspires us to take these risks—and even if we fail, we've still taken another step toward realizing them. In this way, risk should not be seen as an all-or-nothing proposition, but rather one of the most important ways in which we aspire to the vision we have for our companies and ourselves.

In 1997, Apple Computer launched its first major brand advertising campaign in several years. Created by TBWA Chiat/Day, the new "Think Different" campaign celebrated the "creative geniuses" of the twentieth century: Albert Einstein, Martin Luther King Jr., Mohandas Gandhi, Pablo Picasso, Amelia Earhart, and Thomas Edison, to name a few. Artists, peacemakers, inventors, and pioneers, these individuals all had the courage to think in a different way, to challenge the norm, to take a risk. Previously, Apple and TBWA Chiat/Day had collaborated on the legendary "1984" ad, in which one courageous woman took on the Orwellian sameness of a PC world. While the "Think Different" campaign represented a softer approach, the core message was the same: risk takers can change the world.

When it comes to Apple itself, CEO Steve Jobs has embraced the role of risk taker to keep his company in the game—and in the process breathe life into the ailing music industry. The Apple brand is undeniably hip, having achieved cult status and a following among designers and artists. However, as we all know, "cult status" generally translates into "miniscule market share." With only 3 percent of the global computer market, Apple has been a niche player in a universe dominated by Microsoft.

But instead of languishing on the sidelines of the PC game, Apple is redefining itself by taking risks. According to *BusinessWeek*, after the tech implosion of 2000, Jobs told employees that the company would "innovate through the downturn" rather than resort to layoffs. That innovation has led to the gradual transformation of Apple into a "high-end consumer-electronics and services company à la Sony."[4] Coming on the heels of its iPod™ MP3 player, Apple launched the iTunes® Music Store amid great fanfare in April 2003. Not only did iTunes offer easy downloading of music from all five major music labels at 99 cents a song, it promised exclusive tracks from artists and special videos that users could view for free.

Many heralded Apple's service as a savior of the music industry, which, in an attempt to stop illegal file sharing, was filing lawsuits against twelve-year-olds and rolling out cumbersome online services that "rented" music to subscribers. With the introduction of iTunes, it appeared that someone— Jobs—finally got it right. "Consumers don't want to be treated like criminals, and artists don't want their valuable work stolen," he remarked. "The iTunes Music Store offers a groundbreaking solution for both."[5]

By the end of 2003, iTunes would be expanded to Windows® users. This and the earlier release of an iPod for Windows represented another kind of risk for Jobs. "The reason Apple has succeeded in creating elegant, easy-to-use software and hardware is that it has complete control over the design and manufacturing of its products," noted *BusinessWeek*. "But coming out with Windows software, such as iTunes, and hardware, such as the iPod, puts Apple in the same situation as any other third-party developer for the dominant Microsoft platform."[6]

However, while Jobs will face a challenge in developing elegant, easy-to-use products for Windows, the rewards could be huge. "Clearly, Apple will benefit enormously if it boosts its share of the computer market by even 1 percent—such a gain would lift its revenues by nearly a third and increase profits even more," reported *Fortune* on the day iTunes was launched. "In the meantime, if [iTunes] takes off—and computer users of all stripes start buying millions of songs on line each month—that will translate into tens of millions of dollars in new revenues per month for Apple."[7]

Just over four months later, Apple reported that iTunes users had purchased and downloaded more than ten million songs. Looks like "thinking different" is paying off.

Moving Forward

As I write this, the economy has been in a slump for nearly three years, depending on how you define the downturn. In response, companies have slashed costs and lowered investment in an attempt to weather the storm. Considering the current environment, this chapter is as timely as ever—for I believe that in downturns and difficult times, CEOs and other organizational leaders must continue to push their tolerance for risk. Fred Smith founded FedEx in one of the worst economic periods since the Depression; Compaq was launched in 1982 amid a recession; and Wal-Mart opened a record number of stores during the 1991–92 recession.

In a *Business 2.0* piece, Gary Hamel and Erick Schoenfeld argue for the need for continued innovation in difficult times. They observe that cost cutting and innovation avoidance in economic downturns only make companies "smaller, not better." Innovation, combined with courage and prudent investment, will position the leading companies of the future:

*In the midst of hunkering down, we need to remind our-
selves that we are still living in a world pregnant with
possibility. The hard times will end. Billions of dollars in
new wealth will be created. Focus too much on retrench-
ment, and your company will emerge from the downturn weakened, diffident and uncertain of the future.
Manage this period well, and your company will emerge
lithe, impassioned, and raring to go. Those who beat the
bear will be ready to ride the next bull.* [8]

It's true that fear makes us more risk averse, and that some
reckless CEOs have given risk taking a bad name. However,
members of Accountable Organizations understand that, even
during tough times, they need to embrace educated, responsible risk taking to ensure the growth and prosperity of their
companies, as well as the advancement of their careers. These
risk takers are creative, courageous, and conscientious—they
have the faith and will to follow their passion, and they do
their homework. When you make it your mission to be the
vanguard, you put your company on the cutting edge.

BUILDING THE
ACCOUNTABLE ORGANIZATION

1. Do you challenge yourself to take risks in your work and in your relationships with others? To help make that determination, ask yourself the following questions:

   - What is the last completely crazy idea I had?

   - Are there any challenging conversations I've been putting off?

   - What more do I know today about our customers that I didn't know yesterday? How am I applying this knowledge to how I do business?

   - When was the last time I failed?

   This last question should be of particular interest to you. If you haven't "failed" in some respect, it means you've been content to live within your comfort zone.

2. How well do you encourage risk taking among those who look to you for guidance? Solicit feedback from your team regarding how challenged they feel in their job and how confident they feel in taking educated, responsible risks.

3. If you are a team member at an organization with a risk-averse environment, how can you introduce or propose educated, responsible risk taking to your supervisor and/or colleagues?

CHAPTER TEN

SOUTHWEST AIRLINES
Integrating Accountable Organization Principles

The Accountable Organization can sound pretty utopian. Some might say that in the real world of cutthroat competition, most companies are wholly occupied with survival—making their targets, making the stockwatchers happy. Of course, if a company doesn't make money, eventually there will be nothing for stakeholders to have a stake in. But some companies are managing to make the grade financially while staying true to the principles of accountability. In fact, some would argue that their accountable culture makes all the difference.

Southwest Airlines: A Standout in an Industry Under Siege

In chapter 2, I related my personal experience with some apparently nonaccountable thinking at a major U.S. airline—an unfortunate thing, given the precarious position of the industry at the time. Despite an enormous bailout package administered by the federal government, major carriers were still cutting routes and laying off employees a year after the September 11 terrorist attacks. U.S. Airways filed for Chapter 11 bankruptcy protection in August 2002, and United Airlines, the nation's second-largest carrier, followed suit four months later. According to the Air Transport Association of America, the industry's losses topped $10 billion in 2002.

The following year, in a dramatic series of twists and turns, American Airlines narrowly avoided bankruptcy. Just as American's unions agreed to steep pay cuts, the deal was nearly swamped by revelations of a pension trust and retention bonuses exclusively for the airline's executives. Chief Executive Donald Carty publicly apologized for how these plans were communicated, but the damage was done: Carty would resign. After intense, down-to-the-wire negotiations, the unions and American's management agreed to a compromise that would allow the airline to avert Chapter 11. At a press conference to announce the last-minute reprieve, Gerard Arpey, American's new CEO, commented, "It will come as no surprise to anyone that there is a definite need to rebuild trust within our company. Not just between unions and management—but between every member of the AMR family."[1] (AMR is American's parent company.)

How different the picture is at Southwest Airlines. In the midst of the turmoil, the discount carrier has stood out for its avoidance of layoffs and continued profitability. In winter 2003, Southwest boasted thirty consecutive years in the black. With the weak economy and increased insurance and security costs, Southwest faced an uncertain profit picture going forward, but its relative success in the midst of an industrywide crisis is a testament to the company's savvy business strategy—and, according to the airline's employees and executives, to its accountable corporate culture. "To me, we could not have achieved our continued success without the culture, that's for sure," says Colleen Barrett, Southwest's president and COO. According to Barrett, Southwest employees "sign up for us because they have a passion for customer service and because they want to be part of a cause, not part of a company."[2]

What Makes Southwest Different?

This is not an organization facing a crisis of trust. An NPR reporter visiting a departmental party at Southwest notes how the employees swarm around Barrett and co-founder Herb Kelleher, both of whom have dropped by to sample the homemade dishes. "This party is instructive about Southwest Airlines in several ways, not the least of which is the obvious lack of deference shown to Kelleher and Barrett," the reporter observes. "There is no fear, no reticence, no carefully parse toadying going on here." Kelleher credits Barrett with being the main architect of Southwest's unique culture, telling the reporter, "She nurtured and she produced a culture which is truly extraordinary, where people feel cared for. They feel wanted. They feel that they can be individualistic. They don't have to wear masks to work."[3] In my conversation with her, Barrett reiterates that sentiment:

> We talk at Southwest a lot about freedom. We encourage freedom within the workplace and we talk about the various freedoms that we offer, both internally and externally. And one of the neatest freedoms that we offer to our employees, I think, is the freedom to be themselves. I spend a lot of time with new hires talking to them about the fact that they were hired because of their individuality.

Some may dismiss all this as warm-and-fuzziness: nice to have, but not the core reason why Southwest succeeds. But because Southwest is an Accountable Organization—and because it is accountable to its *employees* first—the employees in turn fight tooth and nail for their airline. Southwest calls this the "Warrior Spirit," and it's helped the company weather many a storm. Tales abound of employees taking extraordinary initiative—oftentimes at their own expense—to keep the airline successful. After September 11, concerned employees offered to give up part of their paychecks, donate some of their profit sharing—even give Southwest their tax refunds. Employees created "Pledge to LUV" (LUV being the company's stock symbol), a program in which individuals could donate one to thirty-two hours of salary to the airline through paycheck deductions. It wasn't the first time Southwest's employees had pulled together. Back during the first Gulf War, when skyrocketing fuel prices threatened the airline, a cargo employee came up with the idea for a "Fuel from the Heart" program. Through voluntary payroll deductions, Southwest workers raised money to help defray jet fuel costs.

The passion behind this Warrior Spirit also ensures a stellar corporate reputation and exceptional performance in the marketplace. Southwest's claim of legendary customer service is not inflated: the airline consistently wins accolades for customer satisfaction and safety. In the twenty-plus years since *Fortune* has been issuing its annual list of "America's Most Admired Companies," Southwest has landed in the top ten six times; in 2003, it ranked second. From 1997 through 2000, the company ranked in the top five of *Fortune*'s list of "100 Best Companies to Work For in America."

And for those who believe the proof is in the numbers, in fall 2002 *Money* published a list of the thirty best-performing stocks during the thirty years since the magazine was founded. With an annualized return of 25.99 percent, Southwest topped the list—a $10,000 investment in the airline made in 1972 would be worth $10.2 million in 2002. Wharton finance professor and author Jeremy Siegel told *Money*, "When you think about it, it is absolutely remarkable that Southwest could come out No. 1 despite being in probably the worst industry in America."[4]

People First

There is no ambiguity in the message that Southwest seeks to project: While the airline's paying customers are important, its employees are even more so. Says Barrett,

> We are very up front, even with our passengers, in saying we have three customers at Southwest Airlines, and this is their order of importance: number one is our employee, number two is our passenger, and number three is our shareholder. The philosophy being that if we take care of the employees and make them feel good about who they are, and how they are to be the owners we want them to be, then they're going to deliver the same kind of respect and earn the same kind of trust with their passengers that the company earns from the employees.

At corporate headquarters in Dallas, the corridors are covered with thousands of photos of Southwest employees—snapshots of people with their families, their motorcycles, their pets. Instead of Human Resources, the company has a "People Department," one whose philosophy is to hire for attitude, not credentials. After all, Barrett was Herb Kelleher's legal secretary when he co-founded the airline in 1967.

Furthermore, Southwest's mission statement is in two parts, with the second (and longer) section geared specifically to the airline's employees (see p. 165). When I asked Barrett about Southwest's mission statement, she told an interesting story:

SOUTHWEST AIRLINES' MISSION STATEMENT

The Mission of Southwest Airlines

The mission of Southwest Airlines is dedication to the highest quality of Customer Service delivered with a sense of warmth, friendliness, individual pride, and Company Spirit.

To Our Employees

We are committed to provide our Employees with a stable work environment with equal opportunity for learning and personal growth. Creativity and innovation are encouraged for improving the effectiveness of Southwest Airlines. Above all, Employees will be provided the same concern, respect, and caring attitude within the organization that they are expected to share externally with every Southwest Customer.[5]

It was probably in the early eighties—we never had a mission statement. Herb is a great leader and mentor and coach, but he's not too much into the formulaic way of doing things. He really wasn't too keen on having a mission statement. He's a real visionary, but again, he doesn't like to define things, either. At the time, our VP of People—our human resources department—was just insistent that we have a mission statement, because everyone had a mission statement. She hired a consultant

*to come in and work with our senior management com-
mittee, which was probably twelve or thirteen officers at
the time, and they were going to draft a mission statement. Herb went to the first all-day session . . . and he
fired the consultant at the end of the day.*

According to Barrett, Kelleher then drafted a mission statement, including the longer portion dedicated specifically to
employees. The committee then helped fine-tune the statement, maintaining its focus on employees:

*I think all we were trying to do there was to show that
our commitment to our* employees *was as critically
important as any commitment to our shareholders. And
at the time we hadn't defined the pyramid, where
employees were first, passengers second, and shareholders third. But I think we were already philosophically
there—even though we might not have articulated it—
we were already approaching customer service internally
the same as we were externally. And I suspect that's why
we [created the mission statement] that way.*

Trust, Accountability, and
Integrity at Southwest

"Next to safety, which is first and foremost in our business and
has to be the top priority for everybody, I would say that trust is
the number two priority," Barrett says. "I might surprise you
with this answer, but because we approach customer service

exactly the same way—whether it's internal or external—I place the same degree of importance on the word *trust* whether I'm talking about employees or passengers." And at Southwest, the external customer isn't necessarily always right. Barrett explains:

> *It's all very logical to me, but I think it's sometimes a surprise with some other customer service–driven companies that will say the customer is always right. We don't subscribe to that. And we have said that publicly, too, which has caused me a letter or two! But that is one of the ways that we earn the trust of our employees. I'm not saying that if the employee makes a mistake, and it's a serious enough mistake, that they won't be disciplined or talked to. But I am saying that if the customer was wrong, and if the customer behavior was bad, then I am going to defend and support the employee. We haven't done this often, but we have, on occasion, told a customer that we don't want him or her back on our airline.*

So by naming trust a top priority within the organization—and by backing it up—Southwest shows its employees how much they are valued. As Barrett says, if the airline values and respects its employees, they are going to turn around and do the same for their passengers. They'll stand up for their company, just as they know their company will stand up for them. Trust begets trust.

And when it comes to accountability, it's not surprising to hear that the word has been used at Southwest for many years—long before the concept made the media spotlight.

Accountability has been a featured topic of Herb Kelleher's annual "state of the airline" address to the field. And Barrett herself is continuously engaging employees in discussion on the subject. "To me, accountability is taking responsibility for your own actions—you have to *grade* yourself." She then takes it a step further, noting, "Once you've done that, as a Southwest employee, you are then empowered to hold others accountable for their actions. But you can't do it if you're not doing it with yourself first." And when asked about integrity and what it means to the people of Southwest, Barrett replies,

> One of the things that we talk about and have for thirty years at Southwest is the Golden Rule. I guess because of my background and the way I was raised, to me the Golden Rule taught me ethics and gave me integrity. If you were to walk up to employees at Southwest and ask them if integrity is important, I think their answer would be yes. I think if you asked them to define it, they might say to you that it is practicing the Golden Rule . . . it means doing the right *thing.*

Barrett feels the best way to strengthen integrity among her employees is to trust them to make the right decision on their own:

> I don't like it when [employees] say, "Well, what should I do?" I don't want to give them the answer. I say, "Well, what do you think is the right thing to do?" And that can frustrate the hell out of people, but it gets them to really

think. *And in most cases, when the employee knows that you really mean it—you know, it's not a trick question—I think that brings out the integrity in people. Caring enough to really agonize over a decision. When all is said and done, I want the decision to be made in terms of what is best for Southwest Airlines as a whole, not what is best for me as an individual, what is best for my department, whatever the case may be. Am I doing the right thing with this set of circumstances I've got in front of me? If I am, then I'm using integrity in getting there.*

Leadership and Communication

Barrett shares the belief that there is no one prescription for effective leadership. "The key to being the most effective leader is to build an organization or team with people who want to subscribe to and follow your style, philosophies, and behaviors," she says. "In other words, you can have a great leader at one organization who would be a dismal failure at another." Barrett credits the leadership of co-founder and chairman Herb Kelleher with making Southwest what it is today. (Kelleher turned over the airline's day-to-day operations to Barrett and CEO Jim Parker in June 2001.)

In addition to what has undoubtedly been a sure and cautious hand in directing the airline's financial moves ("We've been managed and led for thirty-two years to realize that we need to be managing for the worst of times during the best of times"), Barrett points to Kelleher's humanitarian leadership.

"Part of the success of Southwest has been because Herb is such an *all-inclusive* person," she says.

> *We wouldn't even have titles here if the world didn't dictate that we have them. In Herb's mind, the team is just sort of all on the same level. He'll ask everyone and anyone for their opinions and their thoughts—I'm not saying that he won't mull it over and make a decision finally on his own, but he's all-inclusive in terms of sharing thoughts and soliciting opinions.*

Barrett's own philosophy on communication has a similar egalitarian bent. She believes that the most important aspect of good communication is to reach out to people in every way possible:

> *You can write five thousand memos, and if the person isn't one who learns or wants to communicate on a piece of paper, you've wasted your time because they won't read it and they won't respond to it. So we overkill: we do things on paper, we do things on e-mail, we do things on video . . . we communicate to death. There is not anyone here who could ever say that he or she doesn't get updated frequently on anything in which they have an interest.*

Southwest also improves communication by requiring that managers spend at least one day per quarter in the field, in a department and with an employee that they don't ordinarily work with. Finally, Barrett is a stickler for timeliness when it comes to internal communication:

We follow the exact same philosophies in terms of turn-around time for our internal communications as we do our external. We have goals, and I really hold people accountable on those. I think that the timeliness of the communication is almost as important as the communication itself. So that's something that I've been almost dictatorial about—I will not excuse late responses.

Defining Your Expectations

When asked about her formula for building an organization like Southwest's, Barrett stresses the importance of defining expectations. As with all things at Southwest, Barrett says that clearly defining expectations is equally important at the internal level as well as the external.

I think one of the reasons that Southwest has such loyalty from its passengers and employees is because we tell people very clearly what they can expect to get from us. And we don't purport to be all things to all people. And we don't make excuses for what we're not. I think one of the reasons that our customers are so accepting about the simplicity of our operation is because we take the time to tell them why we operate differently from other carriers, and why that results in a lower fare to them as the user. Also, I've never thought that any employee should ever be surprised at being disciplined or fired. If they are, that's when I call the supervisor or manager, because they haven't clearly defined what the expectation was.

And not surprisingly, Barrett then returns to the concept of accountability as a critical success factor.

You have to religiously hold yourself accountable first and then hold everyone else accountable. You simply cannot make exceptions to accountability. I have no problem in being able to put the personal feelings about someone on one shelf and the accountability rating of someone's contributions and responsibilities to the company on another. I can—and I think everyone should—be able to look a friend in the eye and say, "You haven't performed to our expectation. I don't like you any less, we can still be friends, but I cannot sit here and sign a merit increase for you or sign promotional paperwork for you because you haven't earned it." I think that the higher up that people move in organizations, the more people want to turn their head. I just don't think you can do that.

It seems simple: Tell people what they can expect from you and what you expect of them. Hold yourself accountable for what's expected of you, and then make sure others do the same. It's as clear a prescription as any for true stakeholdership. As Southwest says, it's a company of people, not planes. People are the airline's most important asset. And how do its employees know this? *Because that's the way they are treated.* It's a simple expression of the integrity that's at the heart of all Accountable Organizations.

BUILDING THE
ACCOUNTABLE ORGANIZATION

1. According to President and COO Colleen Barrett, Southwest's commitment to its employees is "as critically important as any commitment to our shareholders." Do you agree or disagree with this philosophy, and why?

2. At your company, is the customer always right? What are the pros and cons of this position in terms of trust, both external and internal?

3. Think about common customer service issues encountered by employees at your company. Ideally, to what extent should employees be empowered to decide the "right" thing to do in these situations?

4. How clear is your organization about expectations—both in terms of what is expected of its employees and what customers can expect from the company? What is the impact on employee and customer trust?

CONCLUSION

When I started my company in 1994, I wasn't driven by the allure of potential riches. After graduate school and several years as a junior executive in corporate America, I wanted to take the best of what I'd learned and create a company of my own. My idealism knew no bounds: I would lead with brilliance and compassion; customers would bang down our doors; and my employees would feel that their time at FWI was an experience—not just a job.

Of course, as you have observed from the many examples in this book, FWI isn't quite the Edenic organization that I had envisioned. We prospered, but we also encountered the challenges that every company faces—and found ourselves struggling for answers. Then, as I became consumed in my own pursuit of making FWI a financial success, I lost sight of why I started the company in the first place. My relationships and health were suffering because of it.

I stopped and took stock. There had to be a way that I could be successful in *all* the things that were important to me, not just my business. As I searched, a single word continued to surface, one that would later become the foundation of the principles outlined in this book. It appeared again and again, in the writings of Emerson and Jefferson, in spiritual works, in books on successful leadership.

That weighty word is *integrity.* And studying what it means made me realize that somewhere along the way, the principles I believed in had become disconnected from the choices I made. When I reconnected them, my life began to turn around. I could become truly accountable in my relationships with others, and because of that, I was rewarded with trust.

I realized that my company needed the same kind of reconnection. When I began to reassess how and why FWI operated, I must admit I was shocked at the parallels with my personal life. The very same principles of integrity, account-ability, and trust played crucial roles in my experience as an entrepreneur—and, looking farther back, in my experience as a citizen of corporate America.

As I noted in the introduction, creating an Accountable Organization is an ongoing process. But as we've seen from companies such as Southwest Airlines, it's a process worth undertaking—not only because pursuing an ethics-driven organization is the right thing to do, but because it's good business. Accountable Organizations thrive because they have a unique competitive advantage over less principled businesses. Consider this perspective from the late Marvin Bower, legendary McKinsey consultant, author, and strategist:

> *The business with high ethical standards has three primary advantages over competitors whose standards are lower:*
>
> *A business of high principle generates greater drive and effectiveness because people know that they can do the* right *thing decisively and with confidence. When there is any doubt about what action to take, they can rely on the guidance of ethical principles. Inner administrative drive emanates largely from the fact that everyone feels confident that he can safely do the right thing immediately. And they also know that any action that is even slightly unprincipled will be generally condemned.*
>
> *A business of high principle attracts high-caliber people more easily, thereby gaining a basic competitive and profit edge. A high-caliber person favors the business of principle and avoids the employer whose practices are questionable. For this reason, companies that do not adhere to high ethical standards must actually maintain a higher level of compensation to attract and hold people of ability.*
>
> *A business of high principle develops better and more profitable relations with customers, competitors, and the general public because it can be counted on to do the*

right thing at all times. By the consistently ethical character of its actions, it builds a favorable image. In choosing among suppliers, customers resolve their doubts in favor of such a company. Competitors are less likely to comment unfavorably on it. And the general public is more likely to be open-minded toward its actions.

Too often, these values tend to be taken for granted. My point in mentioning them is to urge executives to actively seek ways of making high principle a more explicit element in their company philosophy. No one likes to declaim about his honesty and trustworthiness, but the leaders of a company can profitably articulate, within the organization, their determination that everyone shall adhere to high standards of ethics. That is the best foundation for a profit-making company philosophy and a profitable system of management.[1]

By the way, this passage was written in 1966—long before the era of "infectious greed." Bower's words show that while integrity, accountability, and trust are media hot buttons today, these concepts have always been—and will continue to be—central to professional and personal success.

At the core of Accountable Organizations is integrity—ensuring that stakeholders stand by their values, remain true to their purpose, and seek to make decisions based on what's right. There is a pervasive sense of ownership, supported by systems for accountability and leaders who understand their greater responsibility to the organization as a whole. And at the end of the day, this way of doing business earns and sustains trust.

The Accountable Organization is aspirational—it's a discipline that we practice every day. We'll continue to fall down and get back up in our pursuit of it. Most of the time we'll learn from our mistakes and change course; other times we'll repeat the same blunders again and again despite knowing better. Yet we'll continue down the learning path, knowing that with nearly every challenge we confront, we'll become stronger, wiser, and more effective in building trust among our colleagues and customers. Consider this insight from Peter Senge:

> To practice a discipline is to be a lifelong learner. You "never arrive"; you spend your life mastering disciplines. You can never say, "we are a learning organization," any more than you can say, "I am an enlightened person." The more you learn, the more acutely aware you become of your own ignorance. Thus, a corporation cannot be "excellent" in the sense of having arrived at a permanent excellence; it is always in the state of practicing the disciplines of learning, of becoming better or worse.[2]

I, for one, have learned just how difficult this learning process can be. But I've also found that the rewards are commensurate with the challenge. When you and others commit to embracing integrity, accountability, and trust, the collective result—the Accountable Organization—can transform the business environment and help ensure your company's growth and sustainability. The choice for creating that transformation lies with you.

NOTES

Chapter 1

1. "President Bush Signs Corporate Corruption Bill," press release/transcript of speech issued by the White House press secretary's office, the East Room, the White House, July 30, 2002.

2. Jeffrey M. Jones, "Americans Express Little Trust in CEOs of Large Corporations or Stockbrokers," Gallup News Service, July 17, 2002.

3. "Volcker on the Crisis of Faith," interview by Mike McNamee. BusinessWeek, June 24, 2002, 42.

4. Testimony of Chairman Alan Greenspan at the Federal Reserve Board's semiannual monetary policy report to the Congress before the Committee on Banking, Housing, and Urban Affairs, U.S. Senate, July 16, 2002.

5. Francis Fukuyama, Trust: The Social Virtues and the Creation of Prosperity (New York: Free Press, 1995), 26, 51.

6. Raymond Spencer, chairman and CEO of Kanbay, Inc., interview by author, July 26, 2002.

7. Bob Bingham, CEO of The Little Gym, Inc., interview by author, June 25, 2002.

8. Santo J. Costa, interview by author, March 17, 2003.

9. Robert Levering and Milton Moskowitz, "The Best in the Worst of Times," *Fortune* 145, 3 (February 4, 2002): 60.

10. Daniel Roth, "How to Cut Pay, Lay Off 8,000 People, and Still Have Workers Who Love You," *Fortune* 145, 3 (February 4, 2002): 64.

11. Ibid., 66.

12. Ibid., 68.

13. "Agilent President and CEO Ned Barnholt and CFO Adrian Dillon Discuss Q4 Fiscal 2002 Results," interview posted online at www. agilent.com.

Chapter 2

1. "Treasury Secretary Criticizes Misconduct," *Wall Street Journal,* June 14, 2002.

2. Remarks of Attorney General John Ashcroft at WorldCom press conference, Department of Justice, Washington, DC, August 1, 2002.

3. Quotes are from Bob Bingham, Raymond Spencer, Santo J. Costa, and Dave Wolfenden, respectively.

4. My thanks to Michael Saul, Michelle Saul, and James Newton for this example.

5. John Kadlic, vice president, client services, of Blue Diesel; interview by author, March 6, 2003.

Chapter 3

1. Charles Schwab advertisement, printed in *Newsweek,* December 29, 2002.

2. Charles Schwab commercial, rebroadcast as part of a report on National Public Radio's "Morning Edition," June 11, 2002.

3. The Merrill settlement was included in this total.

4. "SEC, NY Attorney General, NASD, NASAA, NYSE and State Regulators Announce Historic Agreement to Reform Investment Practices," press release, Office of New York State Attorney General

Eliot Spitzer, December 20, 2002. Less than a year later, Grasso would resign amid controversy surrounding his $140 million-plus pay package.

5. Stephen L. Carter, *Integrity* (New York: Basic Books, 1996), 5–6.

6. Ibid., 6.

7. *Ethics* (A Magill Ready Reference Book), consulting ed. John K Roth (Pasadena, CA: Salem Press, 1994), 441.

8. Santo J. Costa, interview by author, March 17, 2003.

9. Center for Academic Integrity, www.academicintegrity.org.

10. *Knox College Student Handbook*, 2002–2003, 35.

11. From www.turnitin.com.

12. Center for Academic Integrity, www.academicintegrity.org.

13. Center for Academic Integrity, "The Fundamental Values of Academic Integrity" (brochure), October 1999, 6.

14. Daniel Roth, "How to Cut Pay, Lay Off 8,000 People, and Still Have Workers Who Love You," *Fortune* 145, 3 (February 4, 2002): 63.

Chapter 4

1. Michael E. Gerber, *The E-Myth Revisited: Why Most Small Businesses Don't Work and What to Do About It* (New York: HarperCollins, 1995), 57.

2. Jim Collins, *Good to Great* (New York: HarperCollins, 2001), 195.

3. Daryl Travis, *Emotional Branding: How Successful Brands Gain the Irrational Edge* (Roseville, CA: Prima Publishing, 2000), 102.

4. Collins, 195.

Chapter 5

1. Robert Bruce Shaw, *Trust in the Balance: Building Successful Organizations on Results, Integrity, and Concern* (San Francisco: Jossey-Bass, 1997), 78.

2. Gordon Shaw, Robert Brown, and Philip Bromily, "Strategic Stories: How 3M Is Rewriting Business Planning," *Harvard Business Review* (May–June 1998): 42.

3. Ibid., 50.

4. Chris Argyris, *Flawed Advice and the Management Trap: How Managers Can Know When They're Getting Good Advice and When They're Not* (Oxford: Oxford University Press, 2000), 40–41.

5. Ibid., 43.

6. Ibid., 159.

Chapter 6

1. Rakesh Khurana, *Searching for a Corporate Savior: The Irrational Quest for Charismatic CEOs* (Princeton, NJ: Princeton University Press, 2002), 69.

2. Robert J. Shiller, "Celebrity CEOs Share the Blame for Street Scandals," *Wall Street Journal,* June 27, 2002, citing ideas from Khurana's *Searching for a Corporate Savior: The Irrational Quest for Charismatic CEOs* (Princeton, NJ: Princeton University Press, 2002).

3. Warren Bennis, *On Becoming a Leader* (Cambridge, MA: Perseus Books, 1989), 3.

4. Daniel G. Goleman, Richard Boyatzis, and Annie McKee, *Primal Leadership: Realizing the Power of Emotional Intelligence* (Boston: Harvard Business School Press, 2002), 3.

5. Peter M. Senge, *The Fifth Discipline: The Art and Practice of the Learning Organization* (New York: Currency Doubleday, 1990), 357.

6. Joseph L. Badaracco Jr., *Defining Moments: When Managers Must Choose Between Right and Right* (Boston: Harvard Business School Press, 1997).

7. Walt Sutton, *Leap of Strength: A Personal Tour Through the Months Before and Years After You Start Your Business* (Los Angeles: Silver Lake Publishing, 2000), 97.

8. David Wolfenden, DMB, interview by author, August 19, 2002.

9. The term *emotional intelligence* was popularized in the late 1990s by Daniel Goleman. In his first book on the subject, *Emotional Intelligence,* Goleman argues that EQ is a better predictor of achievement than IQ. As he defines it, emotional intelligence is "the capacity for recognizing our own feelings and those of others, for motivating ourselves, and for managing emotions well in ourselves and in our relationships" (317). In his model, there are five measur-

able areas of emotional intelligence: self-awareness, self-regulation, motivation, empathy, and social skills. Later empirical work by Goleman and others suggests that emotional intelligence is highly correlated with effective business leadership—greater than IQ, schooling, income, or other more traditional drivers of success.

10. Howard Gardner, *Intelligence Reframed* (New York: Basic Books, 1999), 126–128.

11. Craig Weber, president of Weber and Associates, interview by author, April 24, 2003.

12. Joseph L. Badaracco Jr., *Leading Quietly* (Boston: Harvard Business School Press, 2002), 9.

Chapter 7

1. From Eudora's Web site, www.eudora.com/email/features/moodwatch. html.

2. David Kaufer, "Flaming: A White Paper," June 2000, 5.

3. Craig Weber, president of Weber and Associates, interview by author, April 24, 2003.

4. Ibid.

5. From www.rogen.com, www.goldhaber.com.

6. See my working paper "Trust-Based Marketing: Building Winning Brands with Clarity and Purpose," at www. johnmarchica.com.

7. Theodore Levitt, *The Marketing Imagination,* expanded ed. (New York: Free Press, 1986), 111.

8. Paul Lukas, "Johnson & Johnson: Medicine Men," www.fortune.com, April 18, 2003.

9. Richard Alsop, "Scandal-Filled Year Takes Toll on Firms," *Wall Street Journal,* February 12, 2003.

Chapter 8

1. Craig Weber, president of Weber and Associates, interview by author, April 24, 2003.

2. Douglas Stone, Bruce Patton, and Sheila Heen, *Difficult Conversations: How to Discuss What Matters Most* (New York: Penguin Books, 1999), xvi–xvii.

3. William Ury, *Getting Past No: Negotiating Your Way from Confrontation to Cooperation,* rev. ed. (New York: Bantam Books, 1993), 16.

4. Some of the best work on dealing with organizational conflict is from Chris Argyris, a member of the Harvard faculty with joint appointments in education and business. Through his extensive research on organizational dynamics, Argyris acknowledges the problem of prescriptive, step-by-step advice on dealing with problems between people. He advises uncovering what is below the surface: the things people think but don't say, the mental models we assume as fact but are untested assumptions; the willingness to challenge and be challenged. See also the work of the Harvard Negotiation Project and, specifically, Douglas Stone, Bruce Patton, and Sheila Heen, *Difficult Conversations: How to Discuss What Matters Most* (New York: Penguin Books, 1999), for an excellent guide to handling the most challenging workplace and personal conflicts.

5. Thomas F. Crum, *The Magic of Conflict* (New York: Touchstone, 1987), 49.

6. Kirk Blackard and James Gibson, *Capitalizing on Conflict: Strategies and Practices for Turning Conflict to Synergy in Organizations* (Palo Alto, CA: Davies-Black Publishing, 2002), 4.

Chapter 9

1. John A. Byrne, "The Economic Drag of CEO Funk," www.businessweek. com, February 27, 2003.

2. Jeffrey E. Garten, "Listen Up, Execs: Playing It Safe Won't Cut It," *BusinessWeek,* March 3, 2003, 28.

3. Ibid.

4. Jane Black, "Where 'Think Different' Is Taking Apple," www. businessweek.com, August 5, 2003.

5. "Apple Launches the iTunes Music Store," Apple Computer press release, April 28, 2003.

6. Black, "Where 'Think Different' Is Taking Apple."

7. Devin Leonard, "Songs in the Key of Steve," www.fortune.com, April 28, 2003.

8. Gary Hamel and Erick Schoenfeld, "Why It's Time to Take a Risk," *Business 2.0* (April 2003): 63–68.

Chapter 10

1. "CEO and President Gerard J. Arpey's Press Conference Remarks," American Airlines press release, April 25, 2003.

2. Colleen Barrett, interview by author, March 13, 2003. All remarks by Barrett in this chapter are from this interview.

3. Wade Goodwyn, "Profile: Success of Southwest Airlines," NPR, December 4, 2002.

4. John Birger, "The 30 Best Stocks," *Money* (fall 2002): 90.

5. From www.southwest.com.

Conclusion

1. Marvin Bower, *The Will to Manage: Corporate Success Through Programmed Management* (New York: McGraw-Hill/The Marvin Bower Trust, 1966), 113.

2. Peter M. Senge, *The Fifth Discipline: The Art and Practice of the Learning Organization* (New York: Currency Doubleday, 1990), 11.

BIBLIOGRAPHY

Argyris, Chris. *Flawed Advice and the Management Trap: How Managers Can Know When They're Getting Good Advice and When They're Not.* Oxford: Oxford University Press, 2000.

Arrow, Kenneth J. *The Limits of Organization.* New York: W. W. Norton, 1974.

Badaracco, Joseph L., Jr. *Defining Moments: When Managers Must Choose Between Right and Right.* Boston: Harvard Business School Press, 1997.

———. *Leading Quietly: An Unorthodox Guide to Doing the Right Thing.* Boston: Harvard Business School Press, 2002.

Bennis, Warren. *On Becoming a Leader.* Cambridge, MA: Perseus Books, 1989.

Blackard, Kirk, and James Gibson. *Capitalizing on Conflict: Strategies and Practices for Turning Conflict to Synergy in Organizations.* Palo Alto, CA: Davies-Black Publishing, 2002.

Bower, Marvin. *The Will to Manage: Corporate Success Through Programmed Management.* New York: McGraw-Hill/The Marvin Bower Trust, 1966.

Carter, Stephen L. *Integrity.* New York: Basic Books, 1996.

Collins, Jim. *Good to Great.* New York: HarperCollins, 2001.

Covey, Stephen R., A. Roger Merrill, and Rebecca R. Merrill. *First Things First.* New York: Simon & Schuster, 1994.

Crum, Thomas F. *The Magic of Conflict.* New York: Touchstone, 1987.

Davenport, Thomas H., and John C. Beck. *The Attention Economy.* Boston: Harvard Business School Press, 2001.

DePree, Max. *Leadership Is an Art.* New York: Dell Trade, 1989.

Drucker, Peter. *The Effective Executive.* New York: Harper & Row, 1966.

———. *Innovation and Entrepreneurship.* New York: Harper & Row, 1985.

Fritz, Robert. *The Path of Least Resistance: Learning to Become the Creative Force in Your Own Life.* New York: Fawcett Columbine, 1984.

Fukuyama, Francis. *Trust: The Social Virtues and the Creation of Prosperity.* New York: Free Press, 1995.

Gardner, Howard. *Intelligence Reframed.* New York: Basic Books, 1999.

Gerber, Michael E. *The E-Myth Revisited: Why Most Small Businesses Don't Work and What to Do About It.* New York: HarperCollins, 1995.

Godin, Seth. *Permission Marketing.* New York: Simon & Schuster, 1999.

Goleman, Daniel G. *Vital Lies, Simple Truths: The Psychology of Self-Deception.* New York: Simon & Schuster, 1985.

———. *Emotional Intelligence: Why It Can Matter More Than IQ.* New York: Bantam Books, 1995.

———. *Working with Emotional Intelligence.* New York: Bantam Books, 1998.

Goleman, Daniel G., Richard Boyatzis, and Annie McKee. *Primal Leadership: Realizing the Power of Emotional Intelligence.* Boston: Harvard Business School Press, 2002.

Hamel, Gary, and C. K. Prahalad. *Competing for the Future.* Boston: Harvard Business School Press, 1994.

Kawasaki, Guy, and Michele Moreno. *Rules for Revolutionaries.* New York: HarperBusiness, 2000.

Khurana, Rakesh. *Searching for a Corporate Savior: The Irrational Quest for Charismatic CEOs.* Princeton, NJ: Princeton University Press, 2002.

Levitt, Theodore. *The Marketing Imagination.* New York: Free Press, 1983.

Marshall, Edward M. *Building Trust at the Speed of Change: The Power of the Relationship-Based Corporation.* New York: Amacom, 2000.

Meridith, Geoffrey E., Charles D. Schewe, and Alexander Hiam with Janice Karlovich. *Managing by Defining Moments: Innovative Strategies for Motivating Five Very Different Generational Cohorts—Postwar, Leading-Edge Baby Boomer, Trailing-Edge Baby Boomer, Generation X, and N Generation.* New York: Hungry Minds, 2002.

Pine, Joseph B., and James H. Gilmore. *The Experience Economy: Work Is Theatre and Every Business a Stage.* Boston: Harvard Business School Press, 1999.

Roth, John K., consulting ed. *Ethics.* A Magill Ready Reference Book. Pasadena, CA: Salem Press, 1994.

Senge, Peter M. *The Fifth Discipline: The Art and Practice of the Learning Organization.* New York: Currency Doubleday, 1990.

Shaw, Robert Bruce. *Trust in the Balance: Building Successful Organizations on Results, Integrity, and Concern.* San Francisco: Jossey-Bass, 1997.

Solomon, Robert C., and Fernando Flores. *Building Trust in Business, Politics, Relationships, and Life.* New York: Oxford University Press, 2001.

Sonnenberg, Frank K. *Managing with a Conscience: How to Improve Performance Through Integrity, Trust, and Commitment.* New York: McGraw-Hill, 1994.

Steinberg, Leigh, with Michael D'Orso. *Winning with Integrity: Getting What You Want Without Selling Your Soul.* New York: Three Rivers Press, 1998.

Stevenson, Howard H., and Jeffrey L. Cruikshank. *Do Lunch or Be Lunch.* Boston: Harvard Business School Press, 1986.

Stone, Douglas, Bruce Patton, and Sheila Heen. *Difficult Conversations: How to Discuss What Matters Most.* New York: Penguin Books, 1999.

Sutton, Walt. *Leap of Strength: A Personal Tour Through the Months Before and Years After You Start Your Business.* Los Angeles: Silver Lake Publishing, 2000.

Travis, Daryl. *Emotional Branding: How Successful Brands Gain the Irrational Edge.* Roseville, CA: Prima Publishing, 2000.

Ury, William. *Getting Past No: Negotiating Your Way from Confrontation to Cooperation.* New York: Bantam Books, 1991.

INDEX

accountability: blaming vs.,
19–20; as burden, 21; buy-in,
67, 69; collaboration and, 69;
conflict and, 124, 129; definition of, 52; denial of, 22;
determining of, 18–20;
employee, 67–69; eye-level,
16–17; as guilt, 15–17;
liability and, 20–21; as
ownership, 20–23; percep-
tions about, 16–17; responsibility for choices, 22; at
Southwest Airlines, 162,
167–168

Accountable Organization: aspirational nature of, 179; competitive advantages of,
xxii–xxiv, 177; core values of,

xxiv–xxv; integrity of,
xxiv–xxv; ongoing nature of,
176–177; purpose of, xxv;
risk's role in, 140–142;
Southwest Airlines case
study. *See* Southwest Airlines;
stakeholders in, 24–25;
strategic plan of, xxv–xxvi

acknowledgment, 136
Agilent Technologies, 10–12
American Airlines, 160
Apple Computer, 153–156
Argyris, Chris, 67–68
Arpey, Gerard, 160
Ashcroft, John, 16

Badaracco, Joseph, 82–83, 95
Barnholt, Ned, 10

Barrett, Colleen, 161–162, 164, 167–168, 171–172
behavior: ethics influence on, xvi; unethical, xvi
Bennis, Warren, 76–77
Bingham, Bob, 7
Blackard, Kirk, 136
blaming, 19–20
Bower, Marvin, 177–178
brand: description of, 47–48; reinforcing of, 54
Bridgestone/Firestone, 114–116
Bromily, Philip, 64–65
Brown, Robert, 64–65
burnout, 89
busyness, 21
buy-in, 67, 69, 87, 92
Byrne, John A., 139, 142

Carter, Stephen L., 29–30
Carty, Donald, 160
CEO: as celebrity, 73–74; charisma of, 74–75; communicator role of, 93–94; deal maker role of, 85–86; decision-making challenges for, 82–83; disposition of, 90; hands-on involvement by, 88–89; humanitarian role of, 81–83; manager role of, 88–90; motivator role of, 90–91; passion of, 91; risk taker role of, 86–87; risk taking by, 142–146; sage role of, 83–85; visionary role of, 91–93. *See also* leader
Charles Schwab, 27–28
cheating, 34
chief executive officer. *See* CEO
choices: continuity in making, 40; description of, 21–22

clarity: in communication, 103, 110–111; defining of, 44–49; importance of, 61; testing of, 59–61
coaching role of CEO, 83–84
cognitive bias, 125
collaboration, 69
college: honor system in, 34–35; integrity in, 34–35; plagiarism in, 34–36
Collins, Jim, 50–51, 56
commitment: collaboration's role in, 69; description of, 67; leadership, 94–95
communication: clarity in, 103, 110–111; compassion in, 104–105; consistency in, 103–104, 111–112; during a crisis, 113–116; effectiveness of, 102; e-mail effects on, 99; empathy in, 102; frequency of, 104, 112; guideposts for, 101–105; importance of, xxvi; lack of, xxiii; nonverbal cues, 100; personality type and, 107–109; of purpose, 55; quality of, 100; at Southwest Airlines, 170–171; strategic plan, 66; trust building and, 102, 109–113, 116; of values, 55; of vision, 92
communicator role of CEO, 93–94
company: branding of, 47–48; changes in, 87; conflict in, 19; culture of, 18, 145; elements of, 81; eye-level trust in, 9; growth of, 143; image of, 48; mission of, 39; risk taking in, 87, 144–145; vision of, 39

Compaq, 156
compassion, 104–105
conflict: accountability and, 124, 129; assessment of, 126; confronting of, 123–124; description of, 119–120; difficulty in dealing with, 121–124; emotion in, 129–130; examples of, 120–121, 131–135; feedback regarding, 129; impact of, 127; integrity and, 124; management of, xxvi–xxvii; organizational, 131–135; responses to, 121–122; results of, 136; self-perspective on, 128; trust and, 124; unresolvable, 130–131
conflict resolution: acknowledgment from, 136; action plan for, 126–128; appreciation from, 136; creativity improvements after, 136; description of, 121; example of, 131–135; obstacles to, 127; ongoing nature of, 135–136; opportunity derived from, 136; other person's perspective in, 128–130; outcomes of, 128; preparations for, 124–125; upbringing and experience influences on, 123, 125
conscientiousness, 141–142
consumers, 4
context, 78
core values: description of, xxiv–xxv, 40–41; development of, 51–53; understanding of, 50–51
corporate accountability, 33

corporate executives: CEO. See CEO; greed of, 16; wealth of, 16
corporate greed, 2
corporate responsibility, 2
Costa, Sandy, 9, 32
courage, 141
covenant, 9
creativity: conflict resolution and, 136; risk taking and, 141
crisis, communication during, 113–116
Crum, Thomas, 135–136
customers: attracting of, xxiii; communication with, 112–113; learning about, 85–86; product development contributions by, 85; trust of, 7–8

deal maker role of CEO, 85–86
decision making: ethical, xxii–xxiii; integrity in, 40
discipline, 70
distrust, 5, 132
downturns, 156
due diligence, 152
dynamic capitalism, 140

economic downturns, 156
e-mail: benefits of, 106; censoring of, 97–98; guidelines for using, 106–107; quality of communication in, 99–100; workplace usage of, 106
emotion: in conflict, 129–130; description of, 110
empathy, 102, 125
employees: accountability by, 67–69; as stakeholders, 23–25; burnout of, 89; buy-in

employees, *continued*
from, 67, 69, 87, 92; ethical standards and, xxiv; external commitment of, 67; input from, 49, 92; integrity of, 168; internal commitment of, 67; leadership by, 94–95; mentoring of, 84; performance improvements, 89; retention of, xxiv; risk taking by, 146–148; trust in, 8–9
ethical decision making, xxii–xxiii
ethics: laws vs., xvi–xvii; organizations with, xvii–xviii
expectations, 171–172
experimentation, 87
eye-level accountability, 16–17
eye-level trust, 6–10, 12

failure, from risk taking, 149–156
fear: risk taking and, 157; trust and, 132
FedEx, 156
flaming, 98
Ford Motor Company, 114–116
Fukuyama, Francis, 5

Gardner, Howard, 93
Garten, Jeffrey E., 140, 142
Gates, Bill, 88
Gerber, Michael, 45
Gerstner, Lou, 86, 88
Gibson, James, 136
Glauber, Robert, 29
Golden Rule, 31
Goleman, Daniel, 77
Grasso, Dick, 29
greed, 4, 31–32
Greenspan, Alan, 2, 4
guilt, 15–17

Hamel, Gary, 156
Heen, Sheila, 123
honesty, 39, 105
honor system, 34–36
humanitarian role of CEO, 81–83

Iacocca, Lee, 73, 85
infectious greed, 4
integrity: in business environment, 31–33; characteristics of, 30; in college, 34–35; conflict and, 124; decision making based on, 40; definition of, 29–31, 46, 178; description of, xxiv–xxv, 52, 176; foundation of, 31; importance of, 178; leadership, 83; legislating of, 33–37; maintaining of, 61; media portrayals of, 27–29; operating with, 37–40; responsibility for, 35, 37; role of, 31–33; at Southwest Airlines, 168–169; values and, 39–40
internal commitment: description of, 67; lack of, 70

Jobs, Steve, 154–155
Johnson & Johnson, 113–116
Jung, Carl, 107

Kadlic, John, 22–23
Kaufer, David, 98
Kelleher, Herb, 161–162, 164, 166, 168–170
Khurana, Rakesh, 74
King, Martin Luther Jr., 93

laws: ethics vs., xvi–xvii; purpose of, xvi

leader: coaching role of, 83–84; commitment of, 94–95; communicator role of, 93–94; deal maker role of, 85–86; disposition of, 90; "emotionally intelligent," 91; humanitarian role of, 81–83; integrity of, 83; manager role of, 88–90; mentoring role of, 84; motivator role of, 90–91; passion of, 91; power of, 94; respect for others, 80; risk taker role of, 86–87; sage role of, 83–85; teacher-learner role of, 84; trust of, 84–85; visionary role of, 91–93. *See also* CEO

leadership: accountable, xxiii, xxvi; description of, 71, 76; early lessons in, 78–80; effectiveness of, 78; power and, 77; purpose reinforced by, 56; reflections on, 76–77; responsibility of, xxvi; at Southwest Airlines, 169–170; trust and, 5, 80; values reinforced by, 56

Levitt, Theodore, 109
liability, 20–21

manager role of CEO, 88–90
marketing communications: clarity in, 110–111; consistency in, 111–112; honesty in, 112–113
McCabe, Donald, 34
mentoring role of CEO, 84
Merrill Lynch, 28
mission, 39, 49
money, 31–32, 59

MoodWatch, 97–98
motivator role of CEO, 90–91
Myers-Briggs Type Indicator® instrument, 107–108

O'Neill, Paul, 15–16
organization. *See* Accountable Organization; company
outside-the-box thinking, 145
ownership: accountability as, 20–23; of choices, 22; stakeholder role and, 25

Parker, Jim, 169
Patton, Bruce, 123
performance improvements, 89
personal excellence, 149–150
personality type, 107–109
plagiarism, 34–36
power, 77, 94
purpose: changing of, 55–56; clarity of, 44–49; communicating of, 55; leadership's role in reinforcing, 56; media example of, 43–44; power of, 49–56; self-evaluations, 57–58; strategy and, 53
purpose statement, 53–55

QUALCOMM, Inc., 97–98

Reagan, Ronald, 93
rebranding, 48
reciprocal trust, 36–37
respect, 80
risk: in Accountable Organization, 140–142; description of, xxvii; opportunity derived from, 135–136
risk taker role of CEO, 86–87

risk taking: by CEO, 142–146; concepts associated with, 141–142; due diligence in, 152; by employee, 146–148; examples of, 154–155; by executives, 142–146; failure caused by, 149–156; fear and, 157; lessons learned from, 151–153; opportunities for, 148; success and, 153

sage role of CEO, 83–85
Sarbanes-Oxley Act, 1, 33
Schoenfeld, Erick, 156
securities industry scandals, 27–28
Senge, Peter, 77, 179
Shaw, Gordon, 64–65
Shaw, Robert, 64
Shiller, Robert, 74–75
Siegel, Jeremy, 163
Smith, Fred, 156
Southwest Airlines: accountability at, 162, 167–168; communication at, 170–171; company culture at, 162; customer service at, 163; description of, 161; employees of, 162–166; expectations at, 171–172; integrity at, 168–169; leadership at, 169–170; mission statement, 164–166; stock returns, 163; trust at, 161–162, 166–167; Warrior Spirit at, 162–163
Spencer, Raymond, 6–7
Spitzer, Eliot, 28
stakeholders: educating people to become, 25; employees as, 23–25

stock market boom, 2–4
Stone, Douglas, 123
strategic narratives, 64–66
strategic plan: communication about, 66; importance of, 64; internal commitment to, 66–71
strategic planning: description of, 63; sequence of, 64
students: cheating by, 34, 36; honor system for, 34–36
Sutton, Walt, 85

teacher-learner role of CEO, 84
Travis, Daryl, 53
trust: company example of, 161–162, 166–167; conflict's effect on, 124; with customers, 7–8; definition of, 5; description of, 12; earning of, xxii, 80, 84–85; employee, 8–9; eye-level, 6–10, 12; fear and, 132; honesty and, 105; importance of, 7, 52; leadership and, 80; proving of, 60; public, 5–6; at Southwest Airlines, 161–162, 166–167
trust-based marketing, 109–110, 113
trust building: communication's role in, 102–103, 109–113, 116; description of, 60, 102

United Airlines, 160
Ury, William, 124–125
U.S. Airways, 160

values: aspirational, 51; changing of, 55–56; clarity of, 39; communicating of, 55; core. See core values; definition of, 49;

development of, 51–53; expressing of, 40–41; importance of, 50; integrity and, 39–40; leadership's role in reinforcing, 56; power of, 49–56; self-evaluations, 57–58; statement of, 52
vision: communicating of, 92; definition of, 49; description of, 39; determination of, 91–92; purpose and, 53

visionary role of CEO, 91–93
visionary statement, 53–54, 92
Volcker, Paul, 2

Wal-Mart, 156
Weber, Craig, 94, 101, 105, 121–122
Wolfenden, David, 90
work ethic, 70